# Seeking What Is Above, Tied to What Is Below

Joe Evans

*Seeking What Is Above, Tied to What Is Below*
ISBN: Softcover 978-1-951472-76-4
Copyright © 2020 by Joe Evans

All rights reserved. No part of this book may be reproduced or transmitted in any form or by any means, electronic or mechanical, including photocopying, recording, or by any information storage and retrieval system, without permission in writing from the publisher.

# Dedication

I dedicate this book to you, Cece. You will never fully comprehend the joy you bring your mother and me. I preached the sermons in this book during a year when everything seemed to change. For weeks, then months, you were out of school for quarantine. Free from class, you built a two-story tree house, dug a hole so big you could fit into it, and reminded me daily that there is plenty of happiness to be found in the midst of a viral pandemic. God bless you, precious child.

# Contents

Dedication ............................................................................................. 3

**Part 1: Year 3 Started Out Hard**

Seeking What Is Above, Tied to What Is Below ........................... 11
   Hosea 11:1-11 and Colossians 3:1-1

Strangers and Foreigners on the Earth ......................................... 15
   Isaiah 1:1, 10-20 and Hebrews 11:1-3 and 8-16

Our God Is a Consuming Fire ...................................................... 19
   Jeremiah 1:4-10 and Hebrews 12:18-29

Let Mutual Love Continue ........................................................... 24
   Jeremiah 2:4-13 and Hebrews 13:1-8

Onesimus ...................................................................................... 29
   Jeremiah 18:1-11 and Philemon

Who Gave Himself a Ransom for All ........................................... 33
   Jeremiah 8:18 – 9:1 and 1 Timothy 2:1-7

A Love that Never Ceases ............................................................ 38
   Lamentations 1:1-12 and 2 Timothy 1:1-14

Do Not Wander Away to Myths ................................................... 41
   Jeremiah 31:27-37 and 2 Timothy 3:14 – 4:5

Poured Out ................................................................................... 46
   Acts 7:54-58 and 2nd Timothy 4:6-18

**Part 2: Winter**

In the Company of the Faithful .................................................... 53
   Luke 6:20-31 and Ephesians 1:11-23

The Splendor of this House .......................................................... 57
   2 Thessalonians 2:1-5, 13-17 and Haggai 1:15b – 2:9

The Image of the Invisible God, the Firstborn of All Creation ................ 61
   Jeremiah 23:1-6 and Colossians 1:11-20

Old Dogs and New Tricks .................................................................. 66
   Romans 15:4-13 and Isaiah 11:1-10
A Way Through the Wilderness ......................................................... 72
   Psalm 146:5-10 and Isaiah 35:1-10
Emmanuel ............................................................................................ 77
   Isaiah 7:10-16, Matthew 1:18-25
For A Child Has Been Born for Us ..................................................... 83
   Isaiah 9:2-7 and Luke 2:1-20
Called but not Qualified ..................................................................... 87
   Isaiah 42:1-9 and Matthew 3:13-17
Getting Out of the Way ...................................................................... 92
   Isaiah 49:1-7 and John 1:29-42
Leaving Father Zebedee ...................................................................... 97
   Isaiah 9:1-4 and Matthew 4:12-23
Choose Life ........................................................................................ 103
   Deuteronomy 30:15-20 and Matthew 5:21-37

## Part 3- From the Mountain Top to the Quarantine

From the Mountain to the Valley ..................................................... 111
   Exodus 24:12-18 and Matthew 17:1-9 .......................................... 111
Have Mercy on Us, O Lord .............................................................. 117
   Psalm 51 and Isaiah 58:1-12
Seeking the Light by Night ............................................................... 123
   Numbers 21:4-9 and John 3:1-21
Water at Noon ................................................................................... 128
   Exodus and John 4:5-42
Surely, We Are Not Blind, Are We? .................................................. 134
   Psalm 23 and John 9:1-41
Dry Bones .......................................................................................... 139
   Ezekiel 37:1-14 and John 11:1-45
Who is This? ..................................................................................... 144
   Psalm 118:1-2 and 19-29, Matthew 21:1-11

As Often as You Drink It ...................................................................**148**
    Exodus 12:1-14 and 1 Corinthians 11:23-26

Caiaphas' had a plan .........................................................................**152**
    John 18:1-14

He is Risen!.......................................................................................**157**
    Psalm 114 and Matthew 28:1-10

The Lord is My Shepherd.................................................................**161**
    1 Peter 2:19-25 and John 10:1-10

How Can We Know the Way?...........................................................**166**
    1 Peter 2:2-10 and John 14:1-14

I Will Not Leave You Orphaned .......................................................**172**
    1 Peter 3:13-22 and John 14:15-21

The God of Love and Peace Will Be with You ..................................**177**
    Genesis 1:1-4 and 2nd Corinthians 13:11-13

        The Beginning of the Good News of Jesus Christ **182**
    Psalm 91:9-12 and Mark 1:1-20

A Vaccine Is Not Enough to Save Us ................................................**188**
    Psalm 103:6-14 and Mark 2:1-22

# Part 1: Year 3 Started Out Hard

August of 2019 began my third year serving First Presbyterian Church of Marietta, Georgia as a pastor, and the sermons which follow are those I preached as this third year began. Having grown up in this great church, every Sunday was a gift, and every interaction with the members of this congregation brought me joy. Had I known that the outbreak of COVID-19 was on the horizon, I would have cherished every Sunday when we gathered for worship in-person even more.

The fall of 2019 was not short on tragedy. In the following sermons, you'll hear mention of mass shootings and the response of our city's mayor, Steve "Thunder" Tumlin. While the big global news that would shape my third year at this church had yet to happen, what becomes clear to me looking back over the following sermons is that we are always living in challenging times that warrant the Gospel message.

# Seeking What Is Above, Tied to What Is Below
## Hosea 11:1-11 and Colossians 3:1-11

### Preached on August 4, 2019

I RECENTLY had lunch with two great leaders in our church: Mary Margaret and Clem Doyle. Over the course of lunch, in addition to just catching up and enjoying time together, Clem wanted to know what obstacles I thought we might need to overcome as a church in the next few years. He asked, "What is standing in the way of our progress?"

This was a question I wasn't really prepared to answer, and I've been thinking and talking about it ever since. Buck Buchanan said it best, claiming that the great and obvious obstacle standing in the way of growth, evangelism, and the spread of the Gospel here at First Presbyterian Church are the two front doors.

Most every church has doors like ours. They're nice doors that swing right open. Ours even have someone like Harry Vaughn with a smiling face who will open the doors for you. Still, there are a lot of people out in the world who are afraid to go through them.

Why is that?

I believe it's right there in Colossians, a book which makes it clear that being a Christian demands change. This Christian life requires that we leave behind habits we've grown used to. A requirement of the Christian life is that we don't stay the same as we've always been, so Paul charges us in our second scripture lesson to, "Set your minds on things that are above, not on things that are on earth… Put to death, whatever in you is earthly."

Christians have to be different. We have to change, and change is hard, so not everyone is just going to walk through those doors. Grace abounds and new life is here, but change is required, and change is hard. It's hard for all of us.

I want to do it well. I am a pastor after all. More than that, I want to be a Christian, and I know that our religion calls me to a different standard of behavior modeled on the life of Christ.

What does that look like?

Jesus's first miracle in the Gospel of John took place at a party. When the wine ran out, his mother called on him to do something about it. You remember what he did. He didn't take this opportunity to preach. He didn't scold anyone. He told some people to fill up the great empty vats with water, and he turned the water into wine.

We have to remember that image as we read our second scripture lesson, for when Paul talks about the difference between seeking the things that are above and not things that are on earth, what he's really talking about is the difference between being selfish and being mindful of the needs of others.

He's not talking about being antisocial, but how we can be a loving part of the party. We're not called to be more judgmental or self-righteous, but kinder and more charitable. When we consider what it means to be earthly, we must keep in mind the way of life that Jesus modeled. While Jesus never left the wedding party, there are plenty of Christians who will tell you that to follow Jesus, we must leave having fun behind.

Think about Miss Watson in *Huckleberry Finn*. Miss Watson was telling him about heaven and how he must stop being so bad so that when he dies, he can go to the good place, which she described as a place where "all a body would have to do was to go around all day long with a harp and sing, forever and ever." Hearing that, Huck didn't think much of it.

To make matters worse, he asked Miss Watson if she thought his friend Tom Sawyer would go there. When she said, "not by a considerable sight," Huck was glad to go to the bad place, where there might be more exciting things to do, and at least he'd have a friend. Plenty of people think like Huckleberry Finn.

When they hear what they have to give up, they don't want to change, and the doors of our churches become obstacles that the likes of Huckleberry Finn don't want to go through. And who can blame them? I don't want to play the harp with old Miss Watson either.

Later in the book it becomes even more challenging for Huck. There comes the moment in *Huckleberry Finn* when he makes this very important choice. He's run away with Miss Watson's slave, Jim. The heavy weight of stealing, what Huck and so many others believed was her property, weighs heavily on his shoulders. In an attempt to do what was right, he got a piece of paper and a pencil, "all glad and excited," to tell her that a Mr. Phelps has Jim and will give him up for a reward if she'll just send it. After writing this he said, "I felt good and all washed clean of sin."

He thinks he's finally set his mind on what is heavenly, only, he doesn't send the letter straight off. Instead he lays the paper down and sits there thinking. Mark Twain writes, "He got to thinking over their trip down the river. He could see Jim before him all the time: in the day and in the night-time, sometimes moonlight, sometimes storms; they were a-floating along, talking and singing and laughing." So, after considerable thought, finally Huck said, "All right, then, I'll go to hell," and tore up the letter.

We get confused this way sometimes too. What is it that we must give up? What does it mean to be earthly? What does it look like to seek the things that are above? Only, consider how right-side-up Huckleberry Finn had it when he thought he was doing it all up-side down.

The Gospel does call us to a new way of life.

The Gospel does call us to change, but in reading this passage from Colossians, recognize that the way of life that we are called to is being able to see that Christ is all and in all, even in those society has called property or worse. That's what it means to leave behind what is earthly.

That's what it means to set our minds on things that are above. For down here on the earth we are so often blind to the humanity of our neighbors.

When Paul writes, "Put to death, therefore, whatever in you is earthly: fornication, impurity, passion, evil desire and greed," know that being earthly means gratifying our desires at another's expense. Being earthly means cheating our neighbor as though money were more important than people. Being earthly means using faith to justify slavery or so many other abominations. Being earthly is being foolish with our words. It means saying things like, "I wish they'd just go back where they came from." This phrase and so many like it that we hear more and more these days keeps us tethered to the earth and trapped in the past. It's not just that our words can hurt or be used to demean, devalue, and disempower. It's that it's not where we're from that matters, but where we're going.

We Christians must speak using the language of heaven. Our words must reflect the values of that place where, according to our second scripture lesson, there is no longer Greek and Jew, circumcised and uncircumcised, barbarian, Scythian, slave, or free. We are called to see not only the humanity of our neighbor, but the Christ who dwells within him.

I could see how important it is to live that way as I was checking out at Kroger last Friday evening. It was a hot day. Maybe you remember how hot it was. When I was at Kroger, the woman in front of me had taken off her wig while shopping and put it with her produce in her basket, which she placed on the cashier's conveyor belt. The reason I know that is because the cashier bagged all this woman's groceries from the basket, then got to the wig and said, "Ma'am, you forgot your hair." This was at the busy time of the day in the grocery store and everyone was in there and when that's the case, it's easy to be rude to the cashier. It's easy to forget that Christ dwells within her. But we have to slow down, look her in the eye, value her as person regardless of her station, race, or citizenship status, because she might be the one to hand us back our hair.

"Christ is all and in all," proclaims our second scripture lesson. Remember that and know that how we treat the cashier matters more than whether or not we have beer in our shopping carts. How we treat each other determines whether we are trapped in the prison of selfishness or on our way to the Kingdom of Heaven.

I wish the 21-year-old gunman who walked into Walmart yesterday in El Paso, Texas, killing 20 people and wounding 26 others had thought about that. He didn't.

He didn't understand that what we have done to the least of these, we have done to Him. Consider the one whom we serve. For though He had every right to rub shoulders with kings and queens, instead He washed His disciples' feet. While He could have come to judge the world, instead He came to save it. He ate with sinners, tax collectors, and all God's children, even those we fail to see as precious.

And He still does.

The table is before us. All that is required is that you leave what is earthly behind, and step towards the Kingdom of Heaven. What is required is that you give up on status. For here, all are one. What is required is that you give up on self-righteousness. For here, all is grace. When we all choose to live this way, the doors of our churches become no obstacle, for the grace we receive here is what all people long for.

Amen.

# Strangers and Foreigners on the Earth
## Isaiah 1:1, 10-20 and Hebrews 11:1-3 and 8-16

### Preached on August 11, 2019

MY NEW friend Van Perlberg asked me if I was going to be preaching from the book of Galoshes again this week. I told him that it is Colossians, not Galoshes. And no, that week the sermon was about faith, based on a passage from the book of Hebrews." But what is faith?

According to our second scripture lesson, "Faith is the assurance of things hoped for, the conviction of things not seen." Such a definition as this one broadens the way we think about faith, because we generally confine any talk of faith to the world of religion. In reality, there are all kinds of things we don't know for certain. We just have faith in them.

Take snakes, for example.

Jim and Flora Speed had a snake in the house the week before last. They told me this story knowing they might hear it again, and here it is:

They suspected it was in the catch-all room of their house. Their catch-all room came with a door that opens to the side yard, and do you think Flora needed proof that a snake was in there to avoid going into that room? No. Faith is the assurance of things not seen, and she didn't have to see the snake to know that it was there.

That's faith. It's not faith in God, per say. It's faith in the existence of a snake, but my point is that so often we don't need to know for sure that something is there to act as though it is. That's faith. To act on her belief, all she needed was the rumor of a snake, the shadow of a snake spotted by her husband, and the skin of a snake discovered by a woman named Amanda who came over to catch the snake. Amanda from Animal Control came over to the house. She looked around the room where the snake was thought to be, and she said, "It's under that bookshelf." "How do know that?" Dr. Speed asked. Could she see it? No. Amanda just knows enough about snakes - where they like to live and how they act. So, after removing the books from the bookshelf, Amanda got her reward: a fat, black rat snake that she took back to her own property to reduce the rodent population.

You see, you don't have to know something for certain to be right. That's faith.

You don't have to see something for it to be there. That's faith, and we can apply that way of thinking to understand what faith in God is all about. Do we know for certain that God is at work in the world? Can we see God's hand moving? All we need is to understand better the character of God and we will know well enough what God is doing and where God will probably be, but do we know God as well as Amanda knows snakes?

Maybe not.

It's a story that's been told again and again that a man full of doubts went to visit his pastor in her study. "Pastor, I'm afraid I've lost my faith. I just don't believe in God anymore." His pastor responded, "Tell me about this God you don't believe in, because I'm willing to bet that I don't believe in that God either."

The God described in our second scripture lesson is one who makes promises. Those who embody what it means to be faithful are the ones who believe that once God said it will be done, it will be, regardless of whether or not they can see it in plain sight. Abraham was called to set out for a place that he was to receive as an inheritance, and he set out, not knowing where he was going. Isaac and Jacob were heirs of the same promise but lived their lives in tents. Sarah was barren, but considered him faithful who had promised, even though her husband was as good as dead. And through them [Sarah and Abraham], descendants were born, "as many as the stars of heaven and as the innumerable grains of sand by the seashore."

What is faith in God then?

Is it holding fast to the belief that the Earth was created in seven 24-hour days?

Is it never relenting on the conviction that Moses wrote the first five books of the Bible?

Or is it that Jesus was able to walk on the water?

Believing all those things is just fine; however, do not be confused. Faith in God, as defined by our second scripture lesson, has to do not with some exacting standard of fundamental belief, but the absolute conviction that God has promised us a city. And while we have yet to arrive, while we can't yet see it, we are still on our way there.

Sometimes we make faith out to be some big, high, theological word. It's not. It's tangible. Then, at other times we make faith out to be some backwoods, anti-science word. It's not that either. It's required of all of us, especially today. In our world today, to send a child to school is an act of faith.

A new school year has begun. I've been walking our Lily to school each morning. Her little sister is now going to the magnet school out on Aviation Road, but Lily and I still walk to school together until we get to the corner of the school yard. That's where she stops, gives me a hug, and walks on without me. I stand there and watch until she makes it inside. Most days while I'm standing there, she'll turn around to wave at me. When she does that, sometimes I'm overcome with emotions. I stand there and think about how much I love and care for her. I'll imagine what it will be like to drop her off at college. I stand there staring as she walks into her school and think about all these things that I can't see or control, and I'll pray that God will watch over her and all the other children in that school because ours is a world of uncertainty where anything could happen on any day.

It takes faith for me to let her go.

Only what I learned just last Friday, I'm not sure I've had enough faith! Sara dropped Lily off, and on the way to school she said, "Mama, did you know that when Daddy drops me off at school, he just stands there and stares at me the whole time I'm walking? I know he does, because I turn around on my way to the doors, and wave for him to go on, but he just stands there."

What am I to say about these things?

What I'd say is that too often as a father, I'm more controlled by fear than guided by faith. Of course, it's easy to be afraid as a father. Maybe it's impossible not to be, but we become immobilized and all we want to do is hold our children to our chests. Controlled by terror, we react to the world without hope, and lose sight of the new world that God has promised.

So, don't look to my example.

Look somewhere else.

Look to Abraham, who could have turned back, but kept going.

Look to Isaac and Jacob, who lived their whole lives in tents, but were preparing for something else.

Look to Sarah, who was barren, but never gave up hope.

Look to them and know that while around us is fear, hatred, violence, war, and just walking into Walmart takes courage, those who never fail to believe that a better world is coming and are bold enough to walk on toward it are those who will have their reward.

That's what faith is all about, you see.

Though tempted, surely, they did not settle in and grow used to some reality of fear, terror, death, racism, ignorance, and hatred. No. They were not, nor are we, citizens of this world of shadow, for God has promised us that the light shines in the darkness and the darkness will not overcome it.

This afternoon at 1:00 our mayor, Steve "Thunder" Tumlin, has called on Marietta's churches to assemble in prayer, especially for those cities most recently ravaged by gun violence. He called and asked me to help him pull it together, which I was glad to do, though I'm tempted, like many, to grow frustrated with a society who offers "thoughts and prayers," but not much else. Today I feel differently, though. For if we all just stop to remember that God promises us a new heaven and a new earth, our thoughts are open to a different world than the one we have now, and if we are just bold enough to raise our voice in prayer, than, like the great heroes of our faith, we have called on God to help us make it so. Indeed, He will. So, let us have faith enough to follow.

Amen.

# Our God Is a Consuming Fire
Jeremiah 1:4-10 and Hebrews 12:18-29

### Preached on August 25, 2019

THE AMOUNT of communication we've received from our children's teachers this year has been impressive. Among many other messages, this past week we received one teacher's newsletter which began this way:

*Last week was a very busy week of learning new routines and diving right into this year's assigned concepts and standards. The students have had a lot of new responsibilities and expectations and many have already eagerly been working to take them on. It is important that we, as the community and families that surround these students, frequently encourage them, remind them how much we believe in them, and maintain the high expectations that we know they are capable of achieving.*

I thought this message was quite inspirational, but in light of today's scripture lessons, I'd like to reframe some of her language to what might be even more motivating. I wonder how it would feel to parents if their child's teacher sent home a message like this:

*Your children are in dire need of reform. They stand on the cusp of abject failure and doom, performing so far below their assigned concepts and standards that their minds are like a deep darkness. So, while today my classroom is all gloom, like a tempest, I will drown their misconceptions and pluck up and pull down their laziness. Some might tremble with fear at the sight of me, but parents, please encourage and remind them that my class is a consuming fire to burn up their ignorance, that wisdom might shine out of each one of them.*

I don't imagine such a message would be received well, although again and again this is the message of Scripture. Radical change is necessary. Old habits must be left behind, and there is no time for mincing words. Even Jesus, when he walked the earth said, among other things, "I will separate the wheat from the chaff. I will put a new heart within you." To paraphrase, this is because the heart you have isn't getting you where you need to go! The Prophets, especially, used the same kind of language to describe God's work in the world. Amos spoke of the plumb line used by God to measure the crookedness of our society's walls. Such crookedness will be demolished that we might be rebuilt with justice and righteousness. Malachi said that our God is like a refiner of silver, who will heat us and refine us until we reflect his image, or that He is like a fuller who will scrub us with fuller's soap until all impurity is bleached out.

These are images that are familiar enough in Scripture, but teachers can't talk this way.

Or can you imagine if your doctor looked over your blood work and quoted from the prophet Isaiah: "You have become like one who is unclean, and all your righteous deeds are like a filthy cloth. You are fading like a leaf, and your iniquities, like the wind, are going to take you away." That's just not how people talk, but why?

My sense is that in our world today, it's because parents who received a harsh message from their child's teacher would move their child to a different class as soon as possible. Likewise, we want our doctors to be nice and we'll change doctors if ours isn't. However, where is the line between being nice and tolerating bad behavior?

Where is the line between being kind and mollifying those who are hurting themselves?

Where is the line between lying and telling the truth?

We are a people who need to change, and we live in a world that needs to change. I know it and you know it, but who among us wants to be corrected? Isn't it much nicer to be affirmed?

This week President Trump re-tweeted a quote about himself from Wayne Allen Root who said, "President Trump is the greatest president for Jews and for Israel in the history of the world." According to the Washington Post, encouraged by these accolades, the President said, "I am the chosen one," which is a bold statement. Maybe he's not exactly right about that. However, this is how we all are, in a sense.

Even when reform is needed, we'd rather be patted on the back.

Many gravitate towards affirmation rather than criticism.

What must be addressed are the bad habits that clog our arteries, but we don't want to change our diet. On the road to education, what must be confronted first is the reality of ignorance in a culture of persistent denial, but critical words are hard to hear. I wonder if that's because we believe that we are either wheat or chaff, not both.

That's been a problem of mine for a long time, though I'm learning to deal with it. I left Marietta High School thinking that I was all wheat, though there was plenty of chaff to deal with. I graduated with a 3.7 grade point average.

At first, that sounds pretty good. Then I arrived at Presbyterian College and realized that maybe padding my senior year with two periods of shop class and one of weight training hadn't been such a good idea. I tested right into remedial English where I had to face the reality that there were big holes in my education. For example, I didn't understand how to determine which article, "a" or "an", should go before an adjective or noun. My teacher noticed my ignorance, then suggested I go and get some help from a tutor, and it was a blow to my self-esteem. I faced an important decision then: heed her advice or try to change teachers. You know the right answer here but think about how some people view higher education. I could have just gone back home telling my parents that grandpa was right. The academy's been taken over by the liberals who teach evolution and insist that I use the correct determiners in my sentences.

Jesus said he will be separating the wheat from the chaff, but before we can deal with such a challenge, we must first be assured that we are not the chaff. If the prophets said that we are in need of reform, first we must believe that we are worth reforming. If our God is a consuming fire, first we must know that the hymn has it right: It's our dross that he'll consume and our gold that he'll refine, because our God doesn't want us going up in smoke.

Too many of us can't hear criticism, because when we hit walls in life or make mistakes, we think we're the mistake.

Far too many of us confuse correction with condemnation and refinement with rejection.

That's true.

We think of grades on a test the same way we think of grades on an egg carton. Some are "As", a lucky few "AAs", but once one is labeled as a "bad egg," he's fed to the pigs in the slop bucket. That's not how God deals with His precious children.

Such labeling might make sense with eggs, but don't be confused. It's never that way with God. With God, redemption, not rejection, is always the point. Consider our first scripture lesson. Here we have that great story of Jeremiah the young prophet. He's only a boy. Then God came along and spoke right to him. He gives Jeremiah a special responsibility, to "pluck up and pull down, destroy and overthrow." This job sounds quite violent, unless you understand the character of God, for God treats His people the way a gardener weeds his garden. God looks upon the plot and says, "Sure, there is work to do. Weeds must be pulled, and rocky soil tilled," but God isn't going to reject the garden for its defects. God is going to refine the garden until it bears fruit.

In the book of Hebrews, it's the same story.

In our second scripture reading there is a blazing fire, darkness, gloom, and a tempest. We hear the sound of a trumpet and a voice whose words made the hearers beg that not another word be spoken. The message is terrifying but remember that this message to us comes from God, who doesn't give up on His people.

You see, by the testimony of scripture, what becomes clear is God's intention, which is that we be not condemned, but corrected; not rejected, but refined. Our God is a consuming fire. And knowing His character, what will be consumed?

We fear it will be all of who we are. But, according to Hebrews, it is for the removal of what can be shaken, that what cannot be shaken may remain. This is how we must understand hardship, trials, test scores, doctor's appointments, divorces, and lawsuits.

If life is hard, let us let go of the parts of ourselves that hold us back.

If there are bumps in the road, let them shake off our baggage, not derail our journey.

When we are tried and persecuted, let us give up on our broken ways of doing things to learn something new.

However, to do that, something has to change.

We can't turn back to the old ways. Like the ancient Hebrew people, to have new life we must leave Egypt behind.

To bear fruit, we must allow our weeds to be pulled.

To receive the Kingdom that cannot be shaken, we must allow the removal of what can be shaken that what is eternal might remain.

I believe that's true, and I believe it's just like that for a lot of new parents. It's not all smiles and cuteness, for a baby requires a parent to leave an old life behind. So, when some people call babies little bundles of joy, I don't.

I can think of baptisms that were like trying to baptize a racoon.

I see most babies as wrecking balls who renovate their parents' lives completely.

I think parenthood is something like an old *State Farm Insurance* commercial. This one featured a man who says he's never getting married in one scene, and in the next he's buying a wedding ring. Then he tells his wife in an airplane surrounded by crying babies that they're never having kids, and in the next scene his wife is delivering their first child. As he cleans a crayon drawing off the wall of their house he says, "We're never having another kid," to which his wife responds: "I'm pregnant." The commercial ends with this man who made all these declarations about what he was never going to do, but on the couch surrounded by his wife and children he voices one last never: "I'm never letting go."

If our God is a consuming fire, then a father must often decide whether or not he will allow the motorcycle to be consumed, because there isn't room enough in the garage or his life for that *and* the minivan. Those who go off to school face the same decision. If our God is a consuming fire, will they allow their ego to go up in flames that they might learn more than they already think they know? Will politicians listen and change or just forge on denying mistakes? As we become senior citizens, will we allow our freedom, independence, and our driver's license to go up in flames that we might still hold onto dignity and safety? Our God is preparing us for a new life, so what will we hold onto? Our old life? Our career? Our pride? Our innocence? Our fear? When the earth shakes and the flames come, let go of vanity, so that what cannot be shaken, what is eternal, might remain.

Amen.

# Let Mutual Love Continue
## Jeremiah 2:4-13 and Hebrews 13:1-8

**Preached on September 1, 2019**

THIS SCRIPTURE lesson that I've just read is a good reminder of what we, as Christians, ought to be all about. Before that, the scripture lesson which Linley Estrada read is a good reminder that we, as Christians, have a tendency to stray away from what we ought to be all about. Of course, we're not alone in straying. We all stray.

Consider Kentucky Fried Chicken.

Just the name, Kentucky Fried Chicken, makes the core purpose of this corporation plain. Yet last week they started serving something called "beyond fried chicken." Now I don't know what "beyond fried chicken" is exactly, but while it's fried it's not chicken, and you can just about be certain that it didn't come from Kentucky.

What's next, right?

Despite my qualms, this kind of thing happens a lot. We become unmoored from our anchor. We break loose of our roots. We go off the rails. We stray from the very essence of who we are and what we're supposed to be doing. On the other hand, considering expanding American waistlines, it could be that un-chicken is where we should be going. However, most of the time, straying too far from our core purpose is bad.

So, from time to time we have to be reminded of the point.

That's why various human institutions ritualize the simple and crucial act of stating who they are and what they're all about so as not to forget the main thing. Our youngest daughter, Cece, took taekwondo lessons for a while. She loved it, and in addition to seeing her master various punches and kicks, I loved that every lesson ended the same way. At the end of the lesson, the "Senior Student" who has achieved the most advanced rank in the group, would lead the class in reciting the six tenants of taekwondo. Those tenants are the six defining attributes that every student of taekwondo should embody in their daily life: courtesy, integrity, perseverance, self-control, indomitable spirit, and victory.

At the end of the class all the kids lined up. Cece was in the back standing there in her resting stance, and the senior student faced the rest of the class and yelled out, "Courtesy!" and all the kids repeated, "Courtesy!"

Then, "Integrity!" and all the other kids say, "Integrity!"

Then, "Perseverance!"

Then, "Self-control!"

Then, "Indomitable spirit!" And the little ones in the back would yell, "Indom -mmm - ble spirit!"

It was great. It was all just great because what could be better than closing the lesson with the core, essence, or epitome of who every taekwondo student should be and what every student should be doing? The Cub Scouts do the same, reciting again and again, "I promise, to do my best, to do my duty, to God and my country, to help other people, and to obey the law of the pack." The Boy Scouts begin their meetings with the Scout Oath and Law. I'll bet everyone here who's been involved in scouts could stand and say it. This is why the school day starts with the Pledge to the flag and the baseball game with the National Anthem. We use these rituals to summarize and clarify. It's by these kinds of statements that we hope to make our expectations clear and stay on the right path. That's important to do because every group strays, forgets, and becomes distracted from the main thing.

Cece signed up for taekwondo and the first thing I wanted to know is when she was going to karate chop a board in half, but that's not why they're there. It's about integrity, perseverance, self-control, and the indom – mmm - ble spirit. In the same way, Boy Scouts isn't about merit badges and getting into a good college once you attain the rank of Eagle. Being a doctor is about first doing no harm. Life as a lawyer is centered around defending the Constitution and living by a code of fidelity and truth. But how many are like those preachers who stray from such ideals to make a little more money?

How do you keep a group rooted in its true purpose? You make the true purpose plain and clear again and again: "A scout is trustworthy, loyal, helpful, friendly, courteous, kind, obedient, cheerful, thrifty, brave, clean, and reverent."

That's Scouts. What about Christians?

You go out into the world and ask around a little bit and you may hear the opposite of what we intend. You may hear that a Christian is judgmental, closed minded, self-righteous, fearful, so heavenly minded that he's no earthly good. Like every group in human history we need to keep coming back to the real purpose and the true essence of who we are and what we should be doing. To put it in the language of our first scripture lesson from the book of Jeremiah, we go to broken cisterns that cannot hold water again and again, and so, we must be led back to the fountain of living water again and again.

We need this passage in the book of Hebrews to stay rooted in what we should be doing and how we should be living. We must remain committed to embodying the qualities that Christ modeled, so the author of Hebrews writes: "Let mutual love continue."

"Let mutual love continue." Don't let it stop.

It's as though the author of Hebrews were saying to us, "You've been loved by God, saved by his grace. You've memorized the verse, 'For God so loved the world that he gave his only son…' so don't you accept this love and fail to pass it to your neighbor." Don't put a fence around love so that you love the members of your family who you like, the members of your church who you know, and the people who voted for the same people you did. That's not letting mutual love continue, that's showing the world that Christian love is for some and not for others.

If you think it's bad that some people think taekwondo is about breaking legs or that physicians stray from the Hippocratic Oath, then be disgusted by the Church who has lived in such a way that many in our world are convinced that God's love is for some and not for others.

Hebrew's demands that we let mutual love continue, though we've left people out according to race, fenced in love according to standards of sexuality, and built up an idol that makes God's love look like something that not everyone deserves.

"Let mutual love continue, and do not neglect to show hospitality to strangers, for by doing that some have entertained angels without knowing it." Don't you know that's true?

I was reading in *Atlanta Magazine* last week about a man named Marshall Rancifer who spends his nights helping homeless people. He gives them food, takes them to find medical care, and if needed, when they're ready, into recovery for addiction. According to the article he's helped over 2,000 people get off the streets. But his story started when he himself was homeless and found help and comfort in the shelter at Central Presbyterian Church downtown. We don't often know what's going on in the life of the strangers we meet, but too often our assumption is that they're probably up to no good and should be avoided. The book of Hebrews urges us to entertain the possibility that the ones we call stranger might be an angel poised to change the world or, could even be Christ himself.

"Let mutual love continue. Do not neglect to show hospitality to strangers for by doing that some have entertained angels without knowing it. Remember those who are in prison, as though you were in prison with them; those who are being tortured, as though you yourselves were being tortured," even though it is so easy to forget every last one of them.

They put jails and prisons where they do, way out from the road, near the landfill and under the cover of a hillside so that we won't have to trouble ourselves with the thought of them. However, I saw a picture this week that brought their struggle right into my living room. It was a picture of all the rosaries collected back in 2007 from men and women detained for illegally crossing the border. Of course, it's true that this issue has seen greater press coverage recently, but the problem goes back longer, and the root cause is universal: that men and women filled with hope leave their homes to find a better life.

When I saw the rosaries, their faith became clear, as did their humanity.

"Remember those who are in prison, as though you were in prison with them; those who are being tortured, as though you yourselves were being tortured [for are they not God's children too?]. Let marriage be held in honor by all and let the marriage bed be kept undefiled; for God will judge fornicators and adulterers. Keep your lives free from the love of money and be content with what you have."

Some reflections of scholar and Episcopal priest, Gray Temple helped me to understand this part better: "You come to resemble what you admire. People who admire money get green and crinkly. People who admire computers grow user-unfriendly. People who admire youth get juvenile." I would add that people who can't stop looking will never know satisfaction. On the other hand, says Temple, "People who actively and deliberately admire Jesus Christ come to resemble him." Jesus Christ is the same yesterday and today and forever. Isn't that the point of this whole lesson in Hebrews? Maybe that's the point of our entire religion: that Jesus' life is to be mirrored in you and me. So, as you consider this communion table today, be mindful of the life of the one who has prepared it. He is the one who, though he was the King of Kings, set the table and waits on us as a servant.

This food He has prepared is His body, and this wine is His blood. Both of these He offers that we might know our worth and the worth of our neighbor whom He has prepared it for.

The bill will come, but He has already paid it with His life.

All He asks is that the light that shines in Him, shine also in you and me.

May it be so.

Amen.

# Onesimus
## Jeremiah 18:1-11 and Philemon

### Preached on September 8, 2019

TRUTHFULLY, this is just an incredible day. I look forward to this day all year. I love hearing the bagpipes and the drums. I even love wearing this kilt. Especially, I love seeing the tartans come in. The tartans are the centerpiece of this annual worship service. By all these tartans you can see that this service is a symbol that names matter and that all families are blessed by God. This Kirkin or "Blessing" of the tartan's tradition emerged at a time when only those families who had pledged themselves to British rule had the right to wear their plaid publicly. Only those who had kneeled to the crown were allowed to wear their kilts or to hear their clan's name acknowledged. So, when the Church invites every family to come and be recognized in a worship service, it's a radically defiant thing to do. The tartans, publicly displayed, loudly proclaim that we all matter. On this day, before God we stand as equals, even if the Buchanan's haven't paid their taxes to the crown or the Macintoshes have been organizing a rebellion.

If some have been rendered invisible to the monarchy, God sees them.

God calls them by name. They are His.

This service with all the tartans that processed in and the clans they represent, proclaim the truth that all families and all people matter to God. Furthermore, that word "all" applies even to those who don't have a tartan to hold up.

There's no Evans tartan.

Not an official one anyway.

That's OK. I'm not upset about it. I don't feel ignored. As the senior pastor of First Presbyterian Church of Marietta, Georgia, I don't feel ignored basically ever. I was at dinner with two leaders of our church. We ordered drinks, and I ordered something fancy from the bar. I didn't know how fancy it was, until the waiter brought it out on a tray, with a glass dome over it filled with hickory smoke. As the waiter made his way over to our table, grandly removing the dome, everyone in the restaurant was looking at me. That's when Jesi Allers, our Youth Ministry Consultant says to Tom Clarke, "Like he doesn't get enough attention already!"

That's true. Last Thursday I walked our daughter Lily across the street to drop her off at school. On my way back to the car there was a fair amount of traffic. A lot of parents were dropping off their kids, then rushing to work or to run errands. I was just standing there waiting to cross the street when one woman stopped her car and waved her hand toward me and bowed her head like I was the king. I smiled and waved as I crossed, but what came to me in this moment was a memory from my commute to the church last Monday morning.

I was crossing the Harris Hines Bridge and I heard a whistle blow. The woman in the cross walk right over there on Kennesaw Avenue is so used to cars ignoring her as she crosses the road that she's taken to wearing a whistle around her neck that she blows at people who don't stop for her. This is something that she has to do for her own safety, even in the cross walk. Indeed, I heard her blow it and saw a car narrowly pass her by.

This morning, while so many families have been named and recognized by their tartans, we can't forget that in this world, some are still fighting to be seen. Take Onesimus for example. Our second scripture lesson for today was an entire book of the Bible. It's just one chapter, a short letter written by Paul the Apostle to Philemon, a slave owner who hosted a church in his home, regarding his slave Onesimus, who, according to the law of the land, was Philemon's property. In this letter Paul calls Philemon to remember that by the new order established by Jesus Christ, Onesimus is also his brother. Paul names Onesimus and defends him in this letter but consider the ways of the world.

Imagine those many dinner parties when the guests treated him like a fixture of the dining room. How many people walked by him without greeting him as a fellow human being? To what extent did his owner treat him like a piece of his property? When he ran away, was Philemon more concerned with the wellbeing of his brother or the investment he'd just lost? By calling him "brother" Paul calls all of us to a level of equality still needed in this world. But by simply naming him in this letter, the Apostle Paul has already done something radical, for how many names have been forgotten?

Last Sunday I read an article by the great Judy Elliott who remembered a man named Antoine, who discovered and propagated what became known as the "Centennial" pecan. Celebrated at the Centennial Exposition of 1876 held in Philadelphia, this new variety was praised for size and sweetness, yet horticultural tomes never mention the one who discovered it by name. Why? Because racism has rendered some invisible. The same story is retold when it comes to the greatest of hymns, "Amazing Grace," which we'll sing to end this worship service. We know John Newton wrote the words, but today historians speculate that the tune was one he heard slaves sing for comfort in the belly of the slave ships which he captained.

We've forgotten their names and so many others.

Our nation's history is not always unlike the section of the cemetery where generations of men and women are only represented by one marker, not granite a stone bearing their name. Meanwhile, Paul remembers the name Onesimus. "Formerly he was useless to you, but now he is indeed useful both to you and to me," he wrote to Philemon, and urges that he might welcome him "back forever, no longer as a slave but more than a slave, a beloved brother."

Here we are, so close to the 400th anniversary of the date when the first slaves were brought to this country, and yet some figures are still hidden. Nearly 300 years after the words "All men are created equal" were written in the Declaration of Independence, we have yet to live up to our ideals. We must continue to rise to them, that like clay in the potter's hand, rooted in who we have been, we might be continually be "reworked into another vessel." A more perfect vessel. Today, as we celebrate tradition, history, heritage, and roots by looking back on the past, let us celebrate what is good: the tartans, the bag pipes, and the kilts. But can we leave the haggis behind?

Considering history, we don't need to be confined to all of what once was, for reshaped by the Gospel we can become who Christ intends us to be. We must leave behind blindness to our brother, for still in our world, some are called doctor and others patient.

A good friend of mine, Dr. Jim Goodlet, told me that "patient" is the perfect word, because that's what's required. You must have profound patience as you wait in the waiting room, wait for test results, and wait to hear if the cancer's really gone.

Maybe you saw the comic strip last Thursday. The doctor asked, "How are you sleeping?" Crankshaft responded, "I'm sleeping great Doc. I just dozed off for about two hours in your waiting room."

That may just be the way that it is, but have you ever had a doctor who saw you as a person? Isn't that just as healing as whatever medicine she prescribed?

See your brother then.

That's what Paul writes to Philemon. He's calling on him to see Onesimus as his brother, and he's calling on us to see each other with that same clarity of vision.

This past week a Marietta man faced felony charges after police say he purposely struck the driver of a garbage truck with his car after spitting in his face.

Are we not all worth stopping for?

Are we not all deserving of respect?

That's what this worship service is all about.

These tartans are not unlike those great placards carried by the striking Memphis sanitation workers. They said so simply: "I am a man." That's what this worship service is about. Yes, you are, all of you are. God sees you and we see you. In this place you can hold your head up high with your humanity intact.

You matter here, and that's regardless of what you do for a living or the color of your skin. That's regardless of the amount of money in your pocketbook and the birthdate on your driver's license.

That's regardless of who you love.

That's regardless of how you sing.

That's regardless of the test results or the labels the world puts on you.

Raise your head up high as we've raised up the Tartans, because you matter.

You matter to God.

The road to a better future may be potholed with the indifference of the past but it can be repaved by our empathy. Like clay in the hands of the potter, be reshaped by the Gospel today. Recognize your worth and the worth of your brother and sister who is your own flesh there before you.

Let us all look forward to the moment when we will arise at the sound of God calling our name. He knows it, too, for we all matter to Him.

Thanks be to God.

Amen.

# Who Gave Himself a Ransom for All
## Jeremiah 8:18 – 9:1 and 1 Timothy 2:1-7

### Preached on September 22, 2019

JUST BEFORE the Prayers of the People, we sang "There is a Balm in Gilead." This great hymn is based on our first scripture lesson from the book of Jeremiah, where in desperation the Prophet mourns on behalf of God for the people, saying:

*My joy is gone, grief is upon me, my heart is sick.*

*Is there no balm in Gilead?*

*Is there no physician there?*

*Why then has the health of my poor people not been restored?*

We emphasize such themes this Sunday morning on behalf of our brothers and sisters who are still cheering for the University of Tennessee.

Not really.

This is Scripture. It's not about college football, but I have been struck this season by the Vols. We don't watch much college football in our house; however, back when we lived in Tennessee, my wife Sara, our daughters, and I were all UT fans. When you live in Tennessee you have to be. This has been a difficult season for the Vols.

The first game this season was a loss against Georgia State. Georgie State has only had a football team since 2010. You might have heard that on the day of that game, a boat outside the Knoxville stadium caught fire and sank in the Tennessee River. It's been said that UT's game plan for the game was on that boat. Then the Vols were defeated by Brigham Young University, a historically Mormon school in Salt Lake City not considered a football powerhouse.

After that game a friend of mine sent me a picture of a Mormon missionary in a white shirt and dark pants narrowly outrunning a Tennessee defenseman, which was a good illustration for the second defeat of the season.

Then last week, even though Tennessee was victorious against Chattanooga, still a friend sent me a picture of a man at the Georgia game dressed in a Vols jersey with a bag over his head, embarrassed to show his face. You can imagine that after yesterday's loss to Florida there were many in Knoxville not singing "Rocky Top", but asking, "Is there no balm in Gilead? Will we ever win again? When will we be out of our misery?"

Those are all good and important questions. I'm sure that these are the questions the players on the Marietta High School football team who have been recruited by the University of Tennessee are asking. Such questions also bring me to a point that I believe Scripture makes - a lesson so counter-cultural as to be radically surprising: that winning isn't everything.

I'm sure you've heard that before.

I certainly have, because I've lost at a lot of things. My mother, especially, tried to comfort me by telling me that it's not whether you win or lose but how you play the game. I never believed her. Sometimes I still don't. However, I hope you'll hear me out, especially giving the state of youth sports today. As sports become a more and more important part of the lives of our children and grandchildren and as more and more parents sacrifice their free time, driving hours in the car for travel baseball, travel soccer, or travel volleyball, it becomes important to consider what our kids are learning about the importance of victory.

When some parents take their kids out of school for competitions, what are we teaching them? When their schedules are so packed, what are they learning from us about the importance of rest? As Sunday becomes a day for tournaments, what place has religion in the hierarchy of our lives? While I know that the lessons of teamwork, practice, physical fitness, and hard work are lessons that all parents need to teach their kids, I'm worried that we are also teaching them that winning is all that truly matters, though we serve a Lord who taught that the path to salvation is not through victory, but surrender.

We read in 1st Timothy:

*There is one God.*
*There is also one mediator between God and humankind,*
*Christ Jesus, himself human,*
*Who gave himself a ransom for all?*

This section of First Timothy which makes up our Second Scripture Lesson, goes a long way, using just a few phrases, to describe who this Christ is whom we follow and what he has done for us. Scripture testifies to the King of Kings and Lord of Lords who sat not on a throne but died on a Cross to save us from our sins. Rather than rubbing shoulders with princes, he ate with sinners and still welcomes even the likes of us. While he could have avoided suffering, he embraced it. He teaches that the only way to conquer all is to give everything you have to those whom you love.

According to the Apostle Paul, in the eyes of Christ, all our earthly winning is losing. He was bold to say, "Yet whatever gains I had, these I have come to regard as loss because of Christ." We protestants know, by emphasizing such words, that you can't earn God's love or God's salvation. You just must accept God's grace.

Why, then, do we spend so much time helping our kids become winners?

I worry that we are saying one thing, while doing another, when the truth is so much better than the lie that they may be picking up. While we parent place so much importance on sports with the way we spend our time and our money, I don't love our children because of what they've won. I love them because they're mine.

I might like it, but I don't need them to win. I just want them to be fully who God created them to be. But in our world of constant competition, that's easier said than done.

I saw Palmetto Cheese at the store other day, and I remembered the story of the people who started making it. It's made out of Pawley's Island and was started by a couple who runs a small inn on the beach. When they bought the inn, they focused on the dining room right away. I read all this in an interview, that they bought the inn and noticed that the dining room was stuck in some strange patterns. Once a week they had Thai night.

Maybe like me, you like Thai food, but I don't think anyone goes to Pawley's Island looking for it. The women who cooked in the dining room certainly hadn't been trained in Thai cooking, and so this couple who bought the inn encouraged the cooks in the kitchen to prepare the food they knew. Soon enough, good low country fare was coming out of the kitchen, including the pimento cheese, but first this couple had to accept the reality that an inn on Pawley's Island is just fine being who they were meant to be.

That's a hard lesson to learn, because we live our lives in a competition where we're judged according to someone else's rules. There are competitions on TV where they decide who's the best chef, but remember, you don't have to win on one of those shows to make food worth eating. There are people who make the cover of the magazine, but you don't have to look like one of them to be beautiful. There are all kinds of different churches in this world, but we don't have to be like any of them, we can just be us.

As a church we get caught in the same cycle of winning. We start thinking we have to compete with great big churches in Atlanta who have guitars and drums and lights and sound, but does anyone really drive up to our antebellum sanctuary expecting us to be like one of them? No! God created us and God loves us, and we don't have to win every competition to be a great church or to gain God's love. All we have to do is accept God's grace.

This is such a difficult truth to accept, however. Likely, it's difficult to accept because we've been taught to believe that second place is the first loser.

Now, that might be true in sports, but sports are different than real life, and the Kingdom of God has plenty of room on the medal platform.

First Timothy urges us to pray for everyone.

"Everyone" might sound like too many to us, in this culture of winning. If everyone gets a trophy then what does a trophy really even mean?

I get it.

But Scripture calls on us to pray "for kings and all who are in high positions," not only to pray for the politicians we voted for, because they're all God's children, too. According to First Timothy, God our Savior, "desires everyone to be saved and to come to the knowledge of the truth." "Everyone" sounds like a lot of people, but maybe that's only because we've gotten so used to this idea that only a small number of people are worthy of acceptance and praise, only a set number of people ever get to make the team or get in the game. In the Kingdom of God, everyone is somebody and all have a seat at the table with the King.

Back to the University of Tennessee Volunteers. Did you see the shirts that the marching band wore last Saturday? It was college colors day at Altamonte Elementary School in Altamonte Springs, Florida. One 4th grade student didn't have a college shirt to wear, so he wore an orange shirt, drew UT on a piece of paper and safety-pinned it to his shirt. Some kids in the cafeteria noticed and made fun of him, of course.

That's what kids do. It's wrong, but they do it.

If you don't have the right shirt or the right shoes you take your place outside the bounds of popularity. Having been rejected, this child was devastated.

When his teacher saw the look on his face, she tried to affirm him and lift him up. Gradually, word got out about the child and this shirt he'd made. Somehow or another, eventually, word made it all the way to the University of Tennessee and their Pride of the Southland Marching Band, who took his design and mass-produced it. Every one of them was wearing an orange shirt just like the one that this kid made for himself.

Our kids need to hear that story, too.

They need to hear about the balm our God provides in the moment of rejection, of the Shepherd who walks beside us even when we walk through the Valley of the Shadow of Death, and of the arms of the Almighty who is the wind beneath the wings of eagles. Our kids need to hear about such things because so often it is when we have surely been defeated that we finally reach out to the One who has gained the victory by giving himself as a ransom for all.

Let's stop teaching our children to go after glory, that they might give the glory to God.

Amen.

# A Love that Never Ceases
## Lamentations 1:1-12 and 2 Timothy 1:1-14

### Preached on October 6, 2019

LAST WEEK I was glad to attend a meeting of the Board of Zoning Appeals. I was glad to attend when I first arrived but did not feel glad by the time I left. You may have read in the paper about a new homeless shelter proposed by MUST Ministries. In the past, single men were the face of homelessness. Today, most of those being turned away from the existing MUST shelter when it hits capacity are single mothers with children.

The new shelter is designed to meet their needs.

It will have more rooms where mothers and their children can stay together, but before MUST can break ground, first they must gain approval for their new building. Hence the request to the Board of Zoning Appeals.

This meeting with them was public.

Many people showed up. MUST supporters, including former Governor Roy Barnes, as well as residents who live in the area around the current shelter were there. These residents were there to voice their opposition to the new shelter, for they fear that should the Board of Zoning Appeals grant MUST's request, the problems they encounter already with homeless men and women camping out in the woods near their houses will only grow worse by attracting more homeless people.

To persuade the Board, each side gave impassioned speeches.

All those speeches took a long time, because this board grants a full 20 minutes to each side. That's a long time to listen, I realized, and made a mental note to keep my sermons shorter.

When the Board took a vote, they sided with the residents. I left disappointed, but not entirely because my side lost. The residents made fine points. What disappointed me is that their points were made based on the assumption that even a new shelter will not make our community's problem with homelessness any better.

That's a demoralizing thought and a sad state of affairs.

Thinking that way will make you nearly as depressed as reading our first scripture lesson will. That passage from Lamentations is a very sad one, and I asked Rev. Joe Brice to read it because feeling demoralized is nothing new. Throughout history, people have been brought low by circumstance. What's inspiring is to remember the faith of those who persevered.

This past week in Columbia, Tennessee, a man died who I knew well. He was a member of the church I served there. He was a World War II veteran who, following a mission attempting to destroy Japanese submarines, once spent a long night floating in the Atlantic Ocean when the landing gear of his airplane failed to come down.

That happened when he was 19 years old.

Do you know what I was doing when I was 19 years old?

Some of you do, and so you know it wasn't that.

Considering his strength, it occurs to me how progress has afforded each successive generation just a little bit more safety. Maybe a lot more luxury, which is nice, but it's also dangerous. That's because as less and less is required of us in this modern era, we may also fall into the illusion that less and less is possible.

In our second scripture lesson from the book of Second Timothy, Paul the Apostle calls young Timothy to remember the faith "that lived first in [his] grandmother Lois and [his] mother Eunice" and now, he is sure, lives on in him. Calling young Timothy to look back this way was surely inspiring, for there's a tremendous stock of resilience that awaits us in our history.

Paul calls Timothy to remember the faith of his grandmother and mother.

That's helpful, because if we remember what they made it through, the hardship they endured, and what they finally accomplished, surely we'll find strength enough in ourselves to continue the race that they started.

That's why Paul writes to Timothy "Their faith, I am sure, lives in you. For this reason, I remind you to rekindle the gift of God that is within you."

When Timothy hit a hard time, he needed that reminder.

We all do.

We all need to remember the resilient heroes of the past to gain the strength we need for today. Certainly, that's true for me.

My least favorite chore is making our girls their school lunches. Sara never asks me to help her with it, because I hate making their lunches so much. I especially deplore the most tedious step in the school lunch making process: finding the lids to the Tupperware that their lunches will be packaged in. But thinking back on the lives of my grandparents and great-grandparents, I remember to be grateful that there is food at all.

Just two generations ago was the Great Depression, and among us still are those who survived it. Consider them, and don't tell me we can't make it through whatever challenges we face today. There is strength enough within us to make it through anything, even to endure the toxic political climate we find ourselves in. Some people will tell you that the partisan divide is worse than it's ever been.

That's just not true.

Look back just 150 years ago when the South declared war on the North. How's that for a partisan divide? All we have today are some arguing grown-ups, and if you don't like any of them, then do something about it. At least, take the time to vote. Not everyone does that, even. Why? Because the evil one has convinced some of us that they may as well stay at home, that hope is lost, we're too weak to do anything about it, and that nothing can ever change.

This morning I charge you to remember your grandmothers for a minute and rekindle the gift of God that is within you.

Do you know what I wish would have happened at the Board of Zoning Appeals last week? I wish someone had said, "If we all work together, there won't be homeless people in anyone's' back yard." Based on Scripture and the strength of generations, I know we can put all of this city's men and women and children under a roof, if we'd just try.

In the midst of hardship and trial, we must remember that our God's love is a love that never ceases. He is with us in our darkest hour, and like the sun, He rises up each morning to lead us to a brighter day.

Halleluiah.

Amen.

# Do Not Wander Away to Myths
Jeremiah 31:27-37 and 2 Timothy 3:14 – 4:5

## Preached on October 20, 2019

ALWAYS, BUT especially today, we give thanks to God for Scripture. Scripture holds a central place in our Presbyterian tradition. Many Presbyterian churches are designed like ours, with the pulpit in the center. This placement of the pulpit illustrates not that the preacher is of central importance, but that the Word of God is.

That's why I stand here, front and center.

It's not so that everyone can see or hear me, but so that you and I know the place that God's Word must have in our lives. It must be the focal point and the foundation, bringing light to shadow and clarity to all our confusion.

To stand in this pulpit or to touch that old pulpit Bible that I've just read from is really something wonderful, then. It reminds me that for generations, the words of Scripture have been cherished and passed down, translated and debated. When I touch the worn pages of that newly restored Bible that rested in the pulpit of our Sanctuary so that generations of believers would hear the Word of God, it's as though I'm touching something sacred.

In that old pulpit Bible, a symbol of our faith has been preserved. I'm exceedingly grateful to the family who supported the effort to have it restored and the History Committee who sent it off, as well as the woman who knit together again it's binding by hand.

However, it's not enough for us as Christians to preserve the book.

It's not enough to put it under a glass case where it will be kept safe, well maintained for future generations to admire.

All of that is wonderful, of course, but Scripture is not meant for a museum.

Under a glass case or up on a bookcase is not where we are commanded to keep the Word of God, for as we read from the Old Testament book of Jeremiah in the King James Version:

*I will put my law in their inward parts*

*And write it in their hearts;*

Have you ever thought about what that means?

A wonderful author named Richard Rohr retells a story about Joan of Arc. After defending her home country of France from English domination, she had to stand trial for defying her culture's harsh standards of gender. Representatives of the Church tried her for heresy, because in addition to her unladylike behavior of commanding an army, she said that it was God himself who called her to do it.

That didn't sit well with the religious authorities of the time. The Gospel rarely does, and so they couldn't believe that God would ever command a young woman to do anything besides cook or sew. "What makes you that it was God speaking to you?" they asked. "I heard Him speak in my mind and felt Him lead me in my heart," she said.

Giving little credence to her emotions or the voices inside her head, they accused her of falling victim to the power of her own imagination. Yet, Joan of Arc brilliantly responded, "How else would God speak to me?"

Maybe you've had that same feeling of being led by an inner voice, a sense that the divine was leading you somewhere. Only how do you determine which voice is God's and which isn't? That's why Scripture must reside in our hearts. That's why His commandments must fill our inward parts.

All the time we are asked to make choices.

All the time decisions must be made, and some trust the feeling in their gut, others the little voice inside their head. Still others rely on numbers, metrics, and data, but why not use the account of the great heroes of our faith? Why not listen again to the old stories of God at work in the world to gain an understanding of how God is still at work in our lives today?

Second Timothy warns us against turning away from the truth and wandering away to myths. We can only begin to grasp what is truth and what is myth by knowing the words of Scripture so well that we know the sound of God's voice and the quality of His character. Otherwise, we're set at sea like a ship without a rudder or an anchor, victims to the whims of the most constant and manipulative advertisements the world has ever seen.

Has it happened to you, yet, that you ordered something online and, magically, you find yourself presented with similar products when you open the Facebook app on your phone? I recently ordered some fancy, $8.00 shoelaces. (Yes, I know that you can buy two pairs of shoelaces at Walmart for $2.00, but these are something special.)

I ordered two pairs of these shoelaces from a website called whiskers.com. Ever since then I've seen their advertisements everywhere. They're on my phone and on my computer. It's like someone's been watching me and knows what I'll be tempted to buy. That's because someone is. Of course, the news is even worse.

We know now that once you read an article online, you'll be presented with other articles that you might like. This is convenient and good, so long as you're happy and settled with the world view that you currently have and don't want to be disturbed with a different opinion.

Constantly today the salesmen of products and propaganda are knocking down our door, infiltrating our life, trying to tell us what to buy and even how to think. Considering the aggressive cacophony of myths in our daily lives, how can we know who to listen to?

How can we decide whose advice to take?

Which version of the truth is really the truth?

Sorting through the confusion is easy when we remember the words of Scripture:

*Trust in the Lord with all thine heart.*

*And lean not unto thine own understanding.*

We have to know the Word, you see.

Consider our Call to Worship that was from the Psalms, that God's law makes us wiser than our enemies, or again, Jeremiah, where the Lord looks forward to the day when:

*I will put my law in their inward parts*

*And write it in their hearts.*

To have Scripture in our hearts is crucial, because all around us are myths. All around us and even in our own heads are voices that will lead us towards death and destruction. An author once wrote, "We accept the love we think we deserve." He's right. We also listen to the voices we think have it right and we take the advice of those who speak with confidence, even though they often speak without wisdom. Therefore, we must be careful, because myths can ring true, even when they are empty.

There may be a voice that you hear like that of Orson Welles:

*We're born alone, we live alone, we die alone. Only through our love and friendship can we create the illusion for the moment that we're not alone.*

Illusion? That's a myth. Let me tell you why.

I was standing in line at the Starbucks in the hospital last week with our Music Director, Dr. Jeffrey Meeks. A *Journey* song came on:

*He's tearin' you apart*
*Every, every day*
And Jeffrey started singing:
*Cause he's lovin;*
*touchin' another.*

When it got to the next part, all the *na, na, nu, na, na's*, another guy right behind us jumps right in and starts singing with him. He was with his teenage daughter, and while her dad and Jeffrey were crooning in harmony, she and I had the same embarrassed looks on our faces. Regardless, remember these strangers in line singing together and know that while it's easy to go into the hospital and to think that no one cares that you're there, you're not alone.

Don't believe that you are for a second.

Hear the Word of the Lord:

*And lo, I am with you always, even unto the end of the age.*

Do you know those words?

Are they written on your heart?

You'll be scattered by the wind if they're not.

As Scripture warns:

*For the time is coming when people will not put up with sound doctrine, but having itching ears, they will accumulate for themselves teachers to suit their own desires and will turn away from listening to the truth and wander away to myths.*

Don't you know it's already happening?

So many mistake the words inside their head that tear them apart for the Word of the Lord.

So many mistake the bullies in the hall or on the internet for sound doctrine.

So many listen to what people say and think that they must speak for God but listen to what God has to say: *You are mine, my beloved, and with you I am well pleased.*

Too often we imagine Scripture as full of the harsh words that tell us what not to do. We assume that within those pages we will hear that we're all wrong or undeserving. If that's what you think, then take it down from the shelf to read it, that you might come to know the God who called a woman named Joan to lead an army and was incarnate in a man named Jesus, who gave His life out of love for you.

If we don't know with some certainty that we have God's approval, then we will spend our entire lives trying to earn the world's approval, which we will never get.

Do not wander away to myths.

Do not believe what they say.

Instead, continue in what you have learned and firmly believe - that "Jesus loves me this I know, for the Bible tells me so."

Amen.

# Poured Out
## Acts 7:54-58 and 2nd Timothy 4:6-18

### Preached on October 27, 2019

As you may have read on your bulletin cover, or noticed, based on who wrote our first two hymns, today is Reformation Sunday. This is an annual event when we are invited to remember that moment in 1517 when Martin Luther nailed his 95 Theses to a church door in Whittenburg, Germany. These 95 Theses were his 95 complaints, or issues, with the Roman Catholic Church. He judged many priests in the hierarchy, all the way up to the Pope in Rome, to be to be self-serving, manipulative, and corrupt. He believed that a tradition of buying indulgences, or tickets into heaven, (maybe a good idea for the Annual Stewardship Campaign?) made a mockery of the Gospel. And he was tired of worship services that used too much Latin, rather than the language that people actually spoke and could understand. Can you imagine if everything we did here was in Latin? The result of Martin Luther nailing such complaints on a piece of paper to a church door was no small thing. It resulted in the formation of the Lutheran and Presbyterian Churches, then the Baptist, Episcopal, Methodist, and all the other protestants and nondenominationals.

It inspired new forms of worship, widespread democracy, the first Bibles written in languages that most people actually spoke, and nearly cost Martin Luther his life as he was persecuted for heresy.

Because Martin Luther changed the course of his life, stepping out in faith in an act of protest and defiance, risking his reputation and veering from the course he thought his life would take, the whole world changed and is still changing.

The author Eric Metaxas recently wrote a biography of Martin Luther, titled, *The Man Who Rediscovered God and Changed the World*, which begins with this introduction:

In 1934, an African American pastor from Georgia made the trip of a lifetime, sailing across the Atlantic Ocean, through the gates of Gibraltar, and across the Mediterranean Sea to the Holy Land. After this pilgrimage, he traveled to Berlin, attending an international conference of Baptist pastors. While in Germany, this man became so impressed with what he learned about the reformer Martin Luther that he decided to do something dramatic. He offered the ultimate tribute to the man's memory by changing his own name… not long after the boy's father changed his own name, he decided to change his [young] son's name too, and Michael King Jr. became known to the world as Martin Luther King Jr.

Reformation Sunday is today.

As we remember what is called the Great Reformation, know that what we celebrate is not just an important event in the past. Just this word "reformation" inspires us to remember today the reality that change must happen, and sometimes change can even be good.

Today we celebrate that our lives and our society are being reformed and are also always reforming. That's an important message, because oftentimes we want everything to go according to plan. We get an idea in our head that life will move steadily from one milestone to the next, and that if we stay the course we'll be rewarded. That's not always true, so today let us remember that faithfulness is well exhibited in the disruptions.

Today we celebrate that faithfulness according to the Gospel is not modeled in Pharisees who upheld time-tested traditions with reverence and discipline, but in Christ who toppled the tables set in the Temple.

We celebrate not the Priests who recited their Latin masses to the people, though they didn't understand, but Martin Luther who returned the Gospel to the hands of the people.

We model our lives not on the example of those protestors and police officers who fought to maintain segregation, but in Luther's namesake, Martin Luther King Jr., who preached and preached until segregation ended.

These are examples to be remembered as all of us step into the future, that we be not confined to routine, but led by the Spirit.

From the New Testament book Second Timothy, we find encouragement to do just that in the example of the Apostle Paul. We've read in our second scripture lesson a letter to a young man from a more experienced one who knows a thing or two about changing course. As Paul, the author, neared the end of his life on earth he wrote:

*I have fought the good fight,*
*I have finished the race,*
*I have kept the faith.*

These claims he makes about his life are the same claims we all want to make. We all want to run our race well, but at some point, it feels good to stop running or at least, it becomes a little less exiting to take the next step.

I remember being a teenager and every next step was so exciting. It seemed like everyone wanted to know if I had my driver's license, where I was going to college, what I was doing next. Ours is a society that asks about these things, excited about the beginning phases of life. Unfortunately, then, we often get fearful about what comes after that. Just consider, when's the last time you heard someone ask an older person with that same level of excitement: "Are you looking forward to giving up your driver's license?"

"Have you decided on a retirement home?"

"Have you worked on your will?"

While it is commonplace to be excited about steps towards adulthood, in this letter Paul shines a light on the truth, that with faith we might also be joyful in taking steps beyond adulthood:

*As for me, I am already being poured out as a libation, and the time of my departure has come.*

*I have fought the good fight,*
*I have finished the race,*
*I have kept the faith.*

*From now on there is reserved for me the crown of righteousness, which the Lord, the righteous judge, will give me on that day.*

Sometimes we read these words at the funeral, when it's too late for the departed to reap the full benefit of Paul's example. He shows us by his example that we can't just be thinking about change in the first half of our lives. With faith, Paul shows us that we can look forward to every step. His example shows that reformation and change are continual processes that do not come to full fruition until we breathe our last and receive the crown. So, while it's so good to consider how we'll fill our days up, how can we also pour ourselves out?

What will we do once we've filled up our lives with events, choices, careers, relationships, and furniture?

Some downsize and try to give their stuff to their children.

The problem with that is their kids don't want it.

Recognizing that, my grandmother threatened my mother once, "Cathy, when I die, don't you dare have a yard sale. Don't you dare bring my stuff out of the house and into the front yard for strangers to pick over. If you do, I'll haunt you for the rest of your life!"

Isn't it a terrifying thing to imagine your life spread out on a front lawn for strangers to pick through? Still, that's what happens sometimes. We welcome change and newness for several years, but then the expectation becomes that we settle in.

We want to stay the same.

We try to maintain life as it is, but that is not faith, for God is always leading us beyond where we are to where we might be. His call to us, regardless of age, is to keep running the race.

Many do, others just put everything off until it's too late. That's a sad way to go. It's sad to consider those who are old and bitter, breathing their last breath in an empty house full of regrets. I know people like that. Paul's not immune to bitterness either. The strangest details are left for us in the section that an editor of your Bible may have titled, "Personal Instructions." In verses 9-18, the Apostle Paul says a lot. At the end of his life he lists his grievances:

*Demas deserted me.*
*Crescens and Titus are gone too.*
*I hope Alexander the Coppersmith gets what's coming to him.*
*Only Luke is with me.*

But Paul doesn't have anything good to say about him. Mark might be useful, so Paul asks Timothy to bring him when he comes to visit, as well as the cloak that he left with Carpus at Troas.

This detail about the cloak reminded me of the first time Paul is mentioned in Scripture. He was called Saul then, and he was different. In our first scripture lesson from the book of Acts, we read of one of the lowest points in this account of the history of the early Church. A Disciple named Stephen was stoned. He was the first martyr, and when they dragged him out of the city and began to stone him, the witnesses laid their coats at the feet of a young man named Saul. While tragic, there's something wonderful about remembering this memory when considering the end of Paul's life.

There's something wonderful here, in this simple reminder regarding the cloak for it harkens back to who he once was. From the end of his life shines the light of his glory, but Scripture remembers where he once was so that we might also look back and see Paul the Apostle when he was young and stupid. When we're tempted to venerate him, we can see again that even the Apostle Paul, who has more churches named for him than even Martin Luther, was once an accomplice in something horrible. Even he had to be changed by Christ and then, had to keep on changing.

Life is this great process of reformation, and the best stories we can hear are of those who are still growing up, making mistakes, and learning from them. Don't you remember what it was like in 5th Grade when it seemed like no one would ever forget that you got caught picking your nose in Ms. Cook's class? (I'm not speaking from personal experience or anything.) Regardless of your phase of life, can't you see that it's only just the beginning?

We must keep growing and changing until we have poured out what we've filled our lives with and breathe our last to receive the crown.

That's what Paul was able to tell Timothy.

That's what Paul is telling us.

Keep the faith, through every phase of life.

Don't stop changing or growing, for every step-in life requires that we walk alongside the Lord who leads us through life and beyond it.

Yesterday our own Larissa Dukes quoted a passage read in some Jewish circles in a time of morning:

*When I die give what's left of me away.*
*Love doesn't die, people do.*
*So, when all that's left of me is love,*
*Give me away.*

That's how Paul did it. "I am already being poured out as a libation, and the time of my departure has come," he said. While surely he was afraid, having following Christ all his days, he's ready to follow him down the path just a little bit further.

Are you?

# Part 2: Winter

AS FALL turned to winter, the Marietta High School football team was still playing football. Each Advent, as we anticipate the second coming of Christ and prepare ourselves to celebrate Christmas, our worship space is adorned in blue. Surly there were some who gathered for worship last Advent wondering if the blue was there to celebrate the Marietta Blue Devils as they won the state championships.

I mention this because it's so easy to forget what happened before COVID-19 swept the world. COVID-19 wasn't in our lives as we prepared for Thanksgiving or Christmas, though the racial tensions which reached a fever pitch during the quarantine were already heating up. Regardless of the headlines, even news of COVID-19 must take a back seat to the Good News.

This section begins with a sermon from "All Saints Sunday." This is the Sunday when we name those church members who died in the last calendar year. As their names are read, we remember them, and in light of the Gospel, we celebrate how they live on. That is the Good News which must always take center place in our lives.

# In the Company of the Faithful
Luke 6:20-31 and Ephesians 1:11-23

### Preached on November 3, 2019

ALL SAINT'S Sunday is today, and soon I will read from the list of names printed in the bulletin. This is the list of all church members who died in the last year. Yet, to you and to me, it is much more than a list of names and we will do more than read them. Because these are our people, we cannot read their names without acknowledging their significance. They are husbands and wives, mothers and fathers, brothers and sisters, friends and fellow church members. By saying their names, we summon their faces, we hear their voices, and remember who they were. More than that, today we even go so far as to confess that they are saints. Knowing that while their earthly life is over, today we boldly proclaim that they are not gone.

They are not here as they once were, but they have not disappeared.

They have passed away, but they are not lost.

They have breathed their last, but we will meet them again.

Today is a chance to see why Steinbeck, in *The Grapes of Wrath*, pointed to the truth when he wrote that great Tom Joad speech. This is the speech where, rather than say goodbye to his mother, Tom tells her to keep watch for him:

"I'll be around in the dark – I'll be everywhere.

Wherever you can look – I'll be there.

I'll be in the way kids laugh when they're hungry and they know supper's ready, and when the people are eatin' the stuff they raise and livin' in the houses they build – I'll be there, too."

We're doing more than remembering today, you see. We're acknowledging that they're still here, if in a different way. It's more than legacy, what we're talking about this morning. Of course, legacy is important and meaningful. Every time I cross the Harris Hines Bridge, I think about his legacy etched across this state. There's a mark left on this place by A.D. Little that will last forever, just as every name of this list that we'll read has left a legacy that will be felt for years to come. But we're not just remembering today. We'll name them all, and with their names spoken we acknowledge that they are not here where we can see them, but neither are they gone.

On days like today we remember that the great cloud of witnesses draws near, and we are in the company of the faithful.

That's what inspires the cover on your bulletin.

Those aren't aliens landing. They're saints drawing near.

Last week I read a story about a young English clergyman who served a small congregation. It was his custom at evening services to administer the sacrament of the Lord's Supper to any parishioners who remained at the conclusion of the service. One night, so few stayed that he questioned whether the sacrament should be observed, but he proceeded anyway. In the midst of the liturgy, he read part of the Great Prayer of Thanksgiving. This is a prayer that we will pray this morning too, though ours is slightly a different version:

"Therefore, with angels and archangels and all the company of heaven, we laud and magnify thy glorious name." He paused and read that line again, "With angels and archangels and all the company of heaven…" Then he prayed, "God forgive me. I did not realize I was in such company."

Most of the time we don't realize that we are in such company.

We forget who is with us, and we ignore what they call us to do.

It's so easy to ignore or to look beyond not just the Saints who draw near to us, but the entire company of the faithful.

Today I think of Helen Jones, who died just last Saturday. She should be here with her cute red car, parked illegally right outside our doors on the sidewalk. It's because of her that we're now looking into valet parking. If you like this idea, there's a survey to take on the church website. This effort really did start because of her. When we told her she couldn't park her car in front of the bike rack, she said, "Fine!" and, handing her keys to the nearest Deacon, "If I can't park here, you do it!"

We'd now like to maybe formalize that process a little bit.

Helen Jones was something. If we could hear her speak today, I wonder what she would have us do. If today we remember how the Saints draw close and that we are now in the company of the faithful, what do they want us to know?

Do you remember that moment from the Thornton Wilder play, *Our Town*, when Emily, who so recently died, is in her home as a spirit? Having drawn close to her family, she wishes they would "really look at one another."

"It all goes so fast.

We don't have time to look at one another.

I didn't realize.

So, all that was going on and we never noticed… Wait! One more look. Good-bye, good-bye world. Good-bye, Grover's Corners… Mama and Papa. Good-bye clock's ticking… and Mama's sunflowers. And food and coffee. And new ironed dresses and hot baths… and sleeping and waking up.

Oh, earth, you are too wonderful for anybody to realize you.

Do any human beings ever realize life while they live it… every, every minute?"

In the company of the faithful, I realize that we spend too much time worrying and fail to enjoy. We spend too much time working and forget to love. We spend too much time thinking that we'll have tomorrow, but then tomorrow doesn't always come.

A close friend of mine was in a car accident last week. It was bad, but he walked away without a scratch, as did everyone else involved. But this friend, who was recently named the president of the Fort Worth Chamber of Commerce, took his time getting to his office the Friday after this accident. We often talk, but usually about what meetings he's going to or what meetings I'm going to. Lately there have been many meetings regarding the Fort Worth police officer who shot an unarmed African American woman in her home. Yet, on that Friday after this accident I was telling him how cold it was. Maybe it was 32 degrees outside, only in response I heard my friend say, "It's 14. 14."

"No, it's cold, but not that cold. And what do you know about the weather in Georgia when you're in Texas?" I responded.

He said, "Sorry Joe. I wasn't talking to you. My son just asked me what two times seven is, and after this car accident I'm all about that. That's what I want to be doing. Stopping everything to tell my son that two times seven is 14."

Isn't that what they'd be telling us all to do today?

Isn't that what they all would want us to do?

To enjoy the smell of coffee, and new ironed dresses, and hot baths?

To stop to answer multiplication questions?

To rejoice in these moments that we have, trusting that they who have gained their crown do not need our tears, but only wish us happiness?

Today I wish that we had figured out how to valet cars a little sooner.

We've been focused on many things, but how important it is to really see each other the way one police officer in Fort Worth failed to.

Today, remember that we still have the chance to see each other a little more clearly as the precious gifts that we are to each other. Encouraged by the Saints around us this day, we might spend a little more time doing not what is urgent, but what matters.

Today, do not what seemed important yesterday or this morning, but what Christ and all the company of the faithful would have us do.

Amen.

# The Splendor of this House
## 2 Thessalonians 2:1-5, 13-17 and Haggai 1:15b – 2:9

### Preached on November 10, 2019

THIS READING from the book of Haggai, which is a book we don't often take the time to read, is about a Temple renovation. You probably know a lot more about renovations than I do. This is about all I know: renovations take imagination and vision. Additionally, if you get too deep into the reality of the situation you probably won't ever start, much less finish, so you need people around to protect the dream of what could be.

The easier thing than renovating a house is just buying a house that doesn't need to be renovated. That's an attractive option for a lot of people, but for many people that's just not an option.

It wasn't an option for us when we went to buy our first house in Decatur, and so we bought a dump.

I'm sure you know about Decatur.

Decatur, Georgia is now a very nice place to live. When Sara and I were looking for our first house, many parts of Decatur were very nice, but houses in those parts were out of our price range. A house that was in our price range wasn't in one of those nice parts and wasn't in great shape.

There was no washer or dryer in that house.

There was no dishwasher.

There wasn't even a place to hook such appliances up.

There was a vent over the gas range that sucked up smoke from the frying pans, but that vent didn't take the cooking fumes too far. In fact, I remember trying to figure out why there was grease on the adjoining bathroom wall. Then I removed the mirror and there was the back of the range hood. It just sucked up whatever came off the range and moved it to the bathroom.

That wasn't ideal.

I guess if you like to come out of the shower smelling like you slept at Waffle House, this was the bathroom for you, but for most it wasn't ideal. Yet, here's the thing: we could afford it, and we were crazy enough to believe that we could make something of it.

I had learned to tile floors in a class at Home Depot. Sara can do anything she puts her mind to. My dad's cousin was married to an electrician who offered to donate his labor. There were friends around who offered to help us. Plus, the potential was there. Across the street from the house was a creek and greenspace. There was a Chinese chestnut tree in the front yard. Love is all you really need anyway, so we buckled down and gave it a try.

That was our first house.

Maybe that was something like your first house.

What about the Temple?

The prophet Haggai gathered the people around what remained of the temple and asked, "Who is left among you that saw this house in its former glory? How does it look to you now?"

I like this question.

Most people there probably didn't think there was much to see. The truth is that most likely there were only one or two there that day who could remember what the Temple looked like before the Israelites were taken into exile. Scholars who think about this kind of thing say that only a person in what you might call, "the fourth quarter of life" would have remembered seeing it. The First Temple had been destroyed by the Babylonians, and now they stand at the ruins, sixty years later, most in the crowd having only heard about the Temple's splendor from their grandparents. Now, sixty years later, what did they see?

The gold that decorated the place had been taken to adorn the throne rooms of kings in faraway places.

The Ark that held the remains of the 10 Commandments and what remained of the manna was missing.

The walls, once painted, were rubble.

The Priests, who officiated in the room they called the Holy of Holies, had been killed.

"Who can remember the former glory?" is one good question. Another is, "Who can imagine that such glory will ever return?"

The first night we spent in our house in Decatur, I remember how Sara cried.

I wanted to.

What were we doing in that place?

Would it ever be fit to live in?

Would it ever be the kind of place where we'd want to raise a child?

Yet, in our minds was an idea of what it could be, and together, relying on each other, and the expertise of friends and real professionals, it became our home.

That's what it takes of course:

1. Enough imagination to see beyond what's there to what might be.

2. The knowledge that you're not in it alone.

So, the prophet Haggai does assure the people of both those things:

*"Take courage," says the Lord; "for I am with you."*
*"My spirit abides among you; do not fear."*

*For thus says the Lord of hosts: "once again, in a little while, I will shake the havens and the earth and the sea and the dry land; and I will shake all the nations, so that the treasure of all nations shall come, and I will fill this house with splendor."*

You can't renovate without a dream. To rebuild you must have a dream of what could be, otherwise you won't even start. Nor can you renovate if you're all alone.

I had lunch with an old hockey player last week. He was a defenseman. I asked him what his primary responsibility was as a defenseman on the hockey rink, because being born and raised in the South, I don't know anything about hockey other than that it sounds too cold to be much fun.

He told me that his job was to protect the little guys who skate fast and score the goals.

"They can't play scared, those little guys. So, my job was to watch out for them," he said.

Does God not make the same promise?

Has God not done the same for us in this place?

Has God not restored the splendor of this house?

Today is the day of the annual meeting. It's one Sunday a year when we hear about numbers, budgets, and reports from the church officers. It's not typically something that I look forward to, but today it is. I've been so excited to look through the annual report that you'll receive today, because it is the story of what God has done here during our renovation.

It is an accounting of splendor restored, lives changed, and smiling faces.

It reveals the glory of God at work here, and therefore this annual report is worth noticing.

Like the Ancient Israelites, many churches in this country have a memory. Some call it a Camelot memory of full rugs at the children's sermon, a full choir loft, a full preschool, a full youth program, a full sanctuary on a Sunday morning. I call you to take inventory of what God has done and is doing here. To take a good long look around this place and to rejoice, for our God has honored His promise to us.

He has sustained us by His grace.

He is restoring this house to its former glory and reminding us that "The later splendor of this house shall be greater than the former."

So then, brothers and sisters, what will you do? How will you respond? What do you say?

I say, "If God is for us, who could be against us." And I will listen as He calls on me, as He calls on us all to continue the work to the glory of His name.

Halleluiah!

Amen.

# The Image of the Invisible God, the Firstborn of All Creation
## Jeremiah 23:1-6 and Colossians 1:11-20

### Preached on November 24, 2019

THIS COMING Thursday is Thanksgiving, which makes me think about a lot of things. Especially, Thanksgiving makes me think of something that starts with the letter "t."

That's right: traffic.

There's a lot of traffic on Thanksgiving, but there's always traffic here, in Marietta, every day of the year. Each morning people have places to go, and they need to get there quickly, plus they're usually running late. Not long ago I saw a man brushing his teeth while sitting in traffic.

That's strange, isn't it? But people do strange things while they're sitting in traffic.

Some people listen to books, others text, which isn't safe. Some get uncharacteristically angry. In the heat of traffic, even kind people will honk their horn or employ the use of their middle finger.

People have places to go, and they need to get there quickly, plus they're usually running late. They're thinking about what they have to get to, not necessarily about how low the covered bridge is that they're going under. On the front page of the paper last Friday, once again, was coverage of contraptions being installed to prevent people from driving under the historic Concord covered bridge with their too tall cars or trucks. So often our focus is solely on getting some place fast rather than slowing down to pay attention to the signs telling us to turn around or slow down.

Worse, last Friday was coverage of a teenage driver who drove too fast and lost control of his car, running head-on into a school bus. Luckily no one was hurt too badly but let us heed this warning: When the clock is ticking and the boss is waiting, it seems like getting there on time is a matter of life and death. Should we be too hasty, lives may truly hang in the balance between life and death.

When we see the lights of the sheriff or the police officer, our priorities shift.

Or, pulled over on the side of the road so that the hearse can pass, all at once the meeting we were rushing to isn't so important.

When faced with the lights of the squad car or a funeral procession, practice is back to just kids playing ball in a field. Or maybe you realize all at once that you might lose your appointment with the hairdresser or doctor, but for you there will be another day. The hearse is the sign that not everyone will have that.

At the sight of it in Marietta, everything still stops, and we show our respect to the wife, mother, husband, or son, who is looking straight into the reality that the world as they knew it has ended. Stopping for a funeral procession can be a moment where we see clearly again. No matter how important we think the meeting, errand, or appointment is, at the sight of a funeral procession our priorities shift, and whatever we were rushing to gets back into its proper place in the grand scheme of things, because we'll have the chance to be on time again tomorrow. For someone, there will not be a tomorrow, at least not on this side of mortality.

That kind of realization comes when you stop for a funeral procession.

Coming to church can, in a sense, do the same kind of thing.

What we're doing now can shift our own priorities if we're willing. Each week we have six days of being busy.

In a typical week, we have six days of thinking about ourselves and what we must do, what we need, and who all needs us.

Then Sunday comes, the clock strikes 11:00, and we stop.

When the clock strikes 11:00, we stop to look up from whatever it was that seemed so important to focus on the giver and redeemer of life. We have six days of focus on the world and this one hour to focus on the one who created it. We worry about what must be done. Sometimes our obligations keep us up at night, but here, in this hour, we concentrate on the one who will take us from this world into the next.

It's in a moment like this that we are invited to see clearly.

It's in this sacred hour that our priorities shift back to where they should be: God right here at the top and everything else below. Only, here's the problem - while just about everyone in Marietta still stops for funeral processions, not everyone stops at 11:00.

Not everyone stops to see the world clearly through the lens of hope that our Lord provides, so they go on looking through the lens of fear and anxiety.

Not everyone stops so that their priorities settle back into the order they should, so they go on chasing after momentary contentment.

They go on defining themselves by physical beauty, wealth, or popularity.

They go on dedicating themselves completely to their jobs.

They go on rushing through life and wondering why they feel so empty.

They go on thinking that the whole world rests on their shoulders, forgetting about the one who holds the whole world in His hands.

Every once in a while, we all have to stop to think on such things. If we don't, we're like those who race from one thing to the next, busying ourselves with what seems important while neglecting what is essential. We'll race through life, exhausted, yet failing in our true vocation. The first question in the Shorter Catechism in our book of Confessions is this:

*What is the chief end of man?*

The answer: *Man's chief end is to glorify God, and to enjoy him forever.*

I ask you, is that what you've been doing with your time?

There's wisdom on this subject in the book of Proverbs.

Proverbs 16:25:

*Sometimes there is a way that seems to be right, but in the end, it is the way to death.*

Not everyone stops to think about such things as their true priorities. Few people stop to question the rat race that they're in because everyone else is doing it. Still, it is good and right to step off the hamster wheel to consider whether or not we're getting anywhere. It's good to stop and think, and today we are called to stop and think and consider who is at the top and who is down below on the hierarchy of importance.

We all must stop to think about what's driving us.

There's a moment on the show *Mama's Family* when a young man proclaimed, "I get to know God just fine from the comfort of my bed on Sunday morning. I don't need the church to get through life." Mama responded, "Well, you don't need a parachute to jump out of an airplane either."

Today is an important day, and I'm glad that you're here so that together we can stop, let our priorities shift back into the order that they should always have, and remember that we have been thinking so much about our president and his fate that we may have forgotten that we already have a King.

Today is Christ the King Sunday.

It's a day to stop and think about where we're going, which is important, for we have been walking around like we are the masters of our own lives and kings of our own castles for so long that we may have forgotten that we are God's subjects. We have been rushing so quickly through it all that we might think that the future of this world is all up to us. Only wait a minute to consider the truth that God is God, and we are not. No matter how important the appointment we are rushing to, ultimately our fate rests in God. Because today is Christ the King Sunday, this hour has significance, for here is the reminder that among all the failed shepherds who have promised us the world while leading us nowhere, the creator God raised up for us a righteous branch, the firstborn of all creation. In Jesus all things in heaven and on earth were created and in Jesus all things hold together.

Today is the day for us to pull over to the side of this busy life full of anxiety and false hope to recognize that we have a savior, and in Him we have redemption, the forgiveness of sins.

On the other hand, the world doesn't stop.

Some just keep on driving, and they are like those who drive by the funeral procession, unable to recognize that something important is happening.

He is King of Kings and Lord of Lords, but while some bow before him, others just keep on driving.

He is the image of the invisible God, the firstborn of all creation. But while some marvel at him, there are others who don't have time to stop.

He has rescued us from the power of darkness and transferred us into the kingdom of God's beloved Son, but some of us just keep on driving as though nothing new has happened. Yet to be rescued is worth stopping the car, for to be rescued by God means something. This day declares something about who you are and who I am.

According to the author of Colossians, the Lord "has rescued us from the power of darkness and transferred us into the kingdom of his beloved Son." What this statement would have meant in ancient times is that God has captured us, invaded our territory and taken us to a different place. To be transferred into a different kingdom is something like what happened to the nation of Israel when Babylon invaded and took so many of the people to live in exile. Only here it is Christ who has invaded the world, conquered it, and taken us as God's captives into a new kingdom.

Here we have redemption, the forgiveness of sins.

Here we are not subject to the powers of sin and death.

Here all things visible - thrones, dominions, rulers, or powers - are subject to the King of Kings and Lord of Lords, though far too often we still bow before them. Sometimes we look to them for legitimacy. Sometimes we put our trust in their mortal hands, or worse, in our own, which means doing work that is not ours to do.

There was a quote from a humorist named Robert Benchley in the *Marietta Daily Journal* last week:

*Anyone can do any amount of work, provided it isn't the work he or she is supposed to be doing.* What work is ours, but the work of praise?

What work is His? Everything else.

Rest, then, in the security of his powerful love.

Rest in the hands of the image of the invisible God, the firstborn of all creation. For going through life trying to control, manipulate, and do your will on this earth is no way to spend the short time that we have. My friend Dr. Jim Goodlet quoted another pastor to me this last week. One of the great pastors, "the prince of preachers" as he was called, Charles Spurgeon, once said that "good character is the best tombstone, only carve your name on the hearts of those you love, not on a tombstone." Today, let us remember the one who has carved his name on all our hearts. All praise and glory and honor are His, the image of the invisible God, the firstborn of all creation.

Amen.

# Old Dogs and New Tricks
## Romans 15:4-13 and Isaiah 11:1-10

### Preached on December 8, 2019

As I'm sure is the case in your house, Sara and I have a list of banned words that no one is allowed to say. Our girls aren't allowed to tell anyone to "shut up", nor can they call each other "stupid." Sara requires all of us to use proper grammar, so "ain't" is also banned, and sometimes she gets on to me for telling her what "I'm fixing to do". Apparently "fixing to" is not an acceptable alternative to "about to" in the Queen's English.

This Advent season, I've been thinking about adding another word to the banned list: "never." I'm also considering the fate of the words "can't" and "won't." These are words which people use, though a lot of the time these are words that they must later take back. Certainly, that's how it is with kids.

When a kid says: "I'm never going finish my homework," "I'm never talking to her again," or "I'll never make it," you and I may know well enough how to respond. We might say to them something like, "Even though it looks like it's going to take forever, you can, and you will finish your homework." "Even though you're angry now, your anger will pass, and you'll want to talk with her again." Or, "Yes, rejection is hard, not making the team hurts, and when you're standing at the bottom of the hill it may feel like you're never going to make it to the top, but just start walking and see what happens." Those are all things that adults will say to kids, only what about all the other sayings that are just as defeatist that we adults accept as truth all the time?

Consider how negative are the phrases:

"You can't teach an old dog new tricks."

"Some men you just can't reach."

"A leopard can't change his spots."

"That dog won't hunt."

Or my favorite:

"You can't fix stupid."

These phrases are about things that can never happen. They claim that a dog can reach an age in which it's outlived its adaptability; that some men can never be rehabilitated; that born with certain traits a leopard can never change, as though genetics determine fate. And this leads me to "you can't fix stupid," a phrase which people say as though education were but a pipe dream. While it's true that some things can't be done and some problems will never be fixed, often these phrases accept hopelessness, spread discouragement, reinforce depression, wallow in sadness, and allow the power of evil to have the final word. Yet, who has the final word?

You see, just as Genesis tells us that God spoke all that is into existence, we too must be wary of the power of the words that we use and the worlds which those words create. By our words, will we be so bold as to deny that sometimes miracles happen or that sometimes everything changes, and even those dogs who have been spreading their fleas and promising they'll change while never lifting a finger can, in fact, learn?

That's what happened in the Mr. Roger's movie. I hope you've seen it. It looks like it's all about Mr. Rogers, but it's not. It's actually about a grumpy young man who writes for *Esquire Magazine*. It's 1997 and the journalist, his name is Tom, has gained a reputation for taking down heroes from the pedestals that society has placed them on. He goes looking for the skeletons in Mr. Rogers past, yet the plot of the movie is how Mr. Rogers ends up helping Tom face his. Tom's father was an alcoholic. He was abusive. And as Tom's mother was dying in the hospital, young Tom and his sister had to sit with her to help the doctors make the most difficult decisions regarding the person they loved more than anyone. They, though children, were the ones who had to do it because Tom's father was off with his new girlfriend.

Tom couldn't forgive his father for that kind of negligence. He was angry, and the anger that was born of a difficult childhood was poisoning the rest of his life. That's hard for a man to admit, though it can be a state that he's willing to accept as permanent, as though anger were not an emotion to be talked through but were like spots on a leopard that he can never get rid of. Living with that attitude is dangerous and foolish, not only because his life was off track and he could do something about it, but also because even as his father was dying and now a changed man, Tom couldn't see it.

Why was that?

Why couldn't Tom see something good that was obvious to everyone around him?

It's because Tom had "you can't teach an old dog new tricks" tattooed across his eyeballs. Even when the old dog had changed his ways and gained a heart full of love and remorse, Tom, who lived by words like "can't," "never," and "won't", was blind to the shoots that sprang forth from an old, nearly dead stump.

The prophet Isaiah points us towards that image.

It's a small thing - a common thing - a stump with shoots springing forth.

It's something that we've all seen after cutting down a Bradford pear tree, thinking it gone, only to watch it come back year after year, driving us crazy with its determination to testify to the reality of hope.

The Prophet Isiah says, "look at this shoot, a small thing, and know hope springs forth in bigger things, Hope springs forth all around us!" It does, though, so cluttered by "can't," "won't," and "never," hope can be easy to miss.

It's easy to miss hope.

Isn't that sad?

Something like the Presbyterian College Blue Hose are easy to miss, too. Have you ever heard of them? When there are so many other huge football programs around, an alumnus like me has to point out that Presbyterian College really does have a football program and they really are called the Blue Hose, but they haven't been very successful. In fact, I read in our alumni magazine that Presbyterian College is leaving the Big South Conference. Why are they leaving? Because they lose most all their games.

Now that's a sad thing, but sports at a small, liberal arts college is often a sad thing. If you play sports at Presbyterian College, then most likely you won't play professionally, though graduate Justin Bethel of the Patriots does. Still, if you're on the Presbyterian College Blue Hose, then you can't expect to win a whole lot. And if you're a graduate of Presbyterian College, you just about have to accept that you'll never get into sports the way a Georgia graduate would. Maybe to those who are mourning the loss to LSU, that sounds like a good thing, but back to Presbyterian College.

Just last Wednesday, the feature story in the College Sports Journal came with the headline: "Wrestling History About to be Made at Presbyterian College." This year Presbyterian College is home to the only NCAA Division 1 women's wrestling team. They are set to compete at home for the first time in the history of the program.

This occasion reminds me of something my dad said once. My dad was the south east champion in three cushion billiards. I once asked him how he did it. He said, "Son, if you want to be the south east champion of something, it's good to pick a sport that hardly anyone plays."

You might say that this is the case when it comes to women's wrestling, but I say wait, watch, and listen as history is made. A small liberal arts school is making national news. Now that's different from a big deal football program, but it's still something, and if we're always looking for what's big, we may look right past what's there.

Sometimes hope starts as a small thing, only don't ignore it.

A shoot grows into a tree.

A small light will spread to conquer the darkness.

And love is a power stronger than hate, even if the only place you can feel it is in your own heart. Maybe you know that Senator Johnny Isakson, who holds the distinction of being the only Georgian ever to have been elected to the Georgia House, Georgia Senate, U.S. House, and U.S. Senate, has just stepped down from his office in the U.S. Senate due to ongoing health issues. He is a three-term senator, and because we live in a country of division and partisanship, there's been conflict between Georgia governor Brian Kemp and President Donald Trump over who ought to be appointed to fill his Senate seat until the next election. All that has now been settled and put to rest. What I don't want to put to rest is how Mr. Isakson seized the opportunity in his farewell speech not to celebrate himself or make note of his many accomplishments, but to urge all legislators to "forget their differences and focus on common ground to find solutions" for the good of this country and its people. He went on to highlight his friendship with U.S. Representative John Lewis of Atlanta, pointing to their relationship as an example of the change that bipartisanship can bring if people just let it.

In today's world, that seems like a longshot, and many have already given up on it saying it will ever happen. But during his speech he said, "Bipartisanship will become a way we accomplish things, a way we live, a state of being. It will be the end of a bad time and the beginning of a new one and I'm going to live long enough to see both." He also said, "America is changing for lots of reasons" and the solutions to our problems are in people's hearts.

How's your heart?

Is it hard and cold like Pharaoh's, who would not let God's people leave Egypt?

Is it settled in the way things are now and resistant to how they might be?

Is it open to what God is doing in the world?

Is it prepared to live in a new heaven and a new earth where:

*The wolf shall live with the lamb,*
*The leopard shall lie down with the kid,*
*The calf and the lion and the fatling together?*

A little child will lead us there, and He is coming, but are you ready to follow? He's not grown used to the way things are because he knows how they might be. This child can see newness springing forth all around Him, so he's a permanent resident of the Promised Land and He declares that it is coming soon, but are you ready?

He's something like a tombstone that I saw last week. A tombstone, by design, is hopeless. It's the great sign of what will now not happen, what has ended, and what won't come back. Yet this tombstone declared:

*This memorial is dedicated to the remarkable life of Melvina "Mattie" Shields McGruder. She was born a slave in South Carolina in 1844. At age 6 she was brought to the nearby Shields Farm in what is now Clayton County, Georgia. Her family would endure a five-generation journey that began in oppression and would lead her descendant to become First Lady of the United States of America, Michelle Obama. Theirs is a story of hope.*

Such hope is so vital in our world today, because too many use words like "can't", "won't", and "never" so often that they're residents of a fallen world full of broken hearts, resigned to broken ways and broken habits. If that's true for you, I call on you to look around at your world this morning.

Just last Monday I saw a great, big largemouth bass mailbox on our street wearing a Santa hat and it reminded me that I must allow Christmas to surprise me. Then I saw a picture of a shoot coming out of a stump on a counselor's card last Tuesday and it reminded me that anything can happen and anyone can change, for hope springs forth all around us and we must not grow so used to the ways of a broken world that we are comfortable in it.

As Paul said in our first scripture reading from the book of Romans, and as I've quoted him every Sunday that I've given the benediction:

*May the God of hope fill you with all joy and peace in believing, so that you may abound in hope by the power of the Holy Spirit.*

Old dogs can learn new tricks.

Alleluia.

Amen.

# A Way Through the Wilderness
## Psalm 146:5-10 and Isaiah 35:1-10

**Preached on December 15, 2019**

LAST TUESDAY was the annual church staff Christmas party. This is an event that all of us look forward to, because it is a rare gift to work in a place like this one, where employees feel so appreciated. This year we were welcomed into the home of Helen Hines. We sat at her dining room table, used her polished silver, were waited on by members of the Administration Council, and ate like kings. Then we gathered in her living room, where Santa delivered gifts.

That took a little while because his sleigh was blocking the driveway, so he had to move it first. Eventually we all unwrapped presents (a Christmas bonus), and I was also honored to receive the black tie that I'm now wearing, which celebrates a recent accomplishment. For months I've been learning to ride a unicycle, and this tie has a unicycle on it with the words, "Yeah, I can!"

And I can.

It took a lot of work, which started when I bought a unicycle at a yard sale. The first time I tried to get on it I knew it had been an impulsive decision because I couldn't even sit still on it. Frustrated, I quit for a couple weeks. Then I picked it back up again with greater determination. Last June I finally peddled once or twice without holding on to anything. I was so proud that I called my family out to the driveway for a demonstration. I miraculously repeated the same feat of riding a unicycle for a distance of nearly one yard.

I'll never forget their response: "Was that it?"

Fueled by their encouragement I kept going. I can now ride for about twenty feet. My goal is to ride in our next church talent show in October, but the point I want to make is that many times I wished for a shortcut.

I wish it had been easier.

I wish I hadn't had to fall so often.

I wish I could have learned this new skill a lot faster.

If I could have learned faster, I might have started trying to learn much earlier, but that's the way it is with new things and long journeys. Just as there are falls in the process of learning, so there is a long way between point A and point B, and that long way in between goes by many different names. You can call it practice, purgatory, or adolescence. In Scripture, the point between point A and point B is often called the desert.

The wilderness or the desert is an in-between place.

The Hebrew people wandered in it for 40 years after leaving slavery in Egypt. Forty years is a long time. Typically, it would take a person just eleven days to walk from Egypt to the Promised Land, but the truth is that making it from slavery to freedom takes much longer and there are setbacks along the way. In the same way, the journey between starting and finishing, or not knowing and knowing, is always harder and always takes longer than we want it to.

We fall more often than we want.

We look silly.

We get frustrated.

The road is rocky, so often people give up before they make it, or they just stay right where they've always been, unchanged.

That's true for some when considering going to the Fox Theater to see *The Nutcracker* or something. One thought of the traffic, and we watch it at home. But that's also true for anyone who is trying to change or learn something new, like a new musical instrument. There's a magazine that I love called *Okra*. I love it because it's a magazine that celebrates the South unapologetically, but without being redneck about it. That tone was summed up in the letter from the Editor of last month's issue:

*We don't try to preserve our past to live in it. We preserve it to feel a connection to our ancestors, to learn from the lessons left behind, thereby creating a better future.*

I like that. I also liked an article in that same issue by a guy named Matthew Magee who knows how to play the fiddle. A friend of his asked him to send some instructions, because his brother-in-law, a classically trained violinist, wanted to learn how to play the fiddle, but only if someone could teach him to do it in about ten minutes. Now I expected Matthew Magee to be clear and say, "That's just not how it works. Getting from point A to point B takes a lot of time." Who knows how many hours of practice our own Will Myers had to put in before he learned to play as he does? And to ask him how to master another style would probably take years. (By the way, at our staff

Christmas party, Will ended up with a t-shirt that says, "God's gift to women." But back to the point). To learn how to play something well takes some time in the desert, yet this Matthew Magee said he would send instructions for learning the fiddle in ten minutes. This is what he wrote:

*All he needs to do is hold the bow a little further up, lower the violin-turned-fiddle off the shoulder, kind of slumping over out of classically taught position. Never use vibrato with the left hand, ever; move like he's getting stung by happy bees. Shuffle the fire out of the notes with double stops every now and then holler something random… not quite on pitch, like "tater patch, tater patch" or "had a dog named Rover, when he died, he died all over," with extreme confidence and wild eyes. Always smile like you know something they don't. Be in the moment and feel the vortex of music pulling you in. The objective is to make people feel like something musically strange is happening, because it is. And that's Fiddling 101 by Matthew Jay Magee.* Mr. Magee ended the article by saying, "What this basically means is… make a joyful noise… [for] the woods would be very silent if no birds sang except those that sang best."

Sometimes we never start because the way is hard or we fear failure, but what if the way were easy and filled with song? What if trying were the same as rejoicing and we knew that walking out on a limb were the same as stepping into the fragile space where Christ takes us by the hand? From the Prophet Isaiah we read:

*The wilderness and the dry land shall be glad.*

*The desert shall rejoice and blossom.*

*Like the crocus it shall blossom abundantly*

*And rejoice with joy and singing.*

What the Prophet means here as he addressed the people Israel is that the land in between where they were, exile in Babylon, and where they longed to be, the Promised Land, was not a desert or barren wasteland. In fact, it was no longer a wilderness at all, but more like a forest full of birdsong or like I-75 when you have a *Peach Pass*.

The highway is clear, he says to us today, for the Lord is here, and no traveler, "not even fools," will miss their turn. The redeemed shall walk, the ransomed shall return, and all will make it to Zion with singing. Everlasting joy shall be upon their heads; they shall obtain joy and gladness, and sorrow and sighing shall flee away.

This is an important and crucial message for us, for like the people of Israel, there are so many moments in life where Point A is not where we want to be, but the getting there to Point B keeps our feet planted.

The illiterate person doesn't want to look foolish. He imagines admitting his need will met with shame, so he hides the fact that he can't read, rather than start the long journey towards literacy.

The addict fears facing the truth, so numbs himself to it again.

The soldier longs for home, but even once she lands back on US soil, there's still a long way to go bills, childcare, learning how to get along with her husband again.

Then for others, the journey through the desert is literally that - a desert.

My first job out of college was as a lawn maintenance man, where I met some of those who had done it. They were men from Mexico, who spoke little English, but had literally crossed a desert to cut grass in Buckhead. I cut grass right beside them and drove around with them in a big truck from house to house. One benefit of such a workday was that my Spanish got pretty good, but no matter how good, the jokes were still hard to make. The only time I really made my coworkers laugh was once when I didn't mean to. They were describing the journey through the desert from Mexico into Texas. They told me that it costs about $5,000 dollars to pay a coyote, or guide, to lead you across the border, and still, you might get caught and sent back.

I asked them if you could get your money back if you didn't make it over. That's when they started laughing. Then I said, "But don't you get a receipt or something?" For the rest of that week my coworkers were retelling my joke to every Mexican lawn maintenance worker they saw, which points to a reality: going from Point A to Point B is a risk.

It's hard.

It costs something.

Only let me say this: The Lord is with us as we walk our pilgrim journey and if we have hope in our hearts then a desert crossing or a mountain pass is nothing.

Consider the Von Trapp family who illegally crossed the Alps into Switzerland to escape the Nazis. For them, the hills were alive with the sound of music.

That's what the Prophet is saying.

*The wilderness and the dry land shall be glad,*

*The desert shall rejoice and blossom;*

For the difference between Point A and Point B is nothing considering how the Son of God bridges heaven and earth, born in a manger, as the great sign that God is with us.

Too often we imagine that he's waiting for us at the finish line and he'll meet us just as soon as we're good enough, or that he'll shake our hand once we have made it in this world. That's not how it works, you see. In the Christ child, we know that he's running beside us in the race, and that even when we slow down, he's right by our side.

Back in Tennessee I went to visit a woman named Mrs. Cotham. Mrs. Cotham was in hospice. I went to visit her and asked her if she was afraid. "I'm not afraid of death," she said. "It's what happens between now and then that scares me."

I can understand.

There's always fear between Point A and Point B.

So, this Advent may our prayer be like that of the great Episcopal priest Thomas Merton, who was bold to pray:

*My Lord God, I have no idea where I am going. I do not see the road ahead of me. I cannot know for certain where it will end. [Yet I do know this,] you will lead me by the right road though I may know nothing about it. Therefore, I will trust you always though I may seem to be lost in the shadow of death. I will not fear for you are ever with me, and you will never leave me to face my perils alone.*

"Do not fear, for I am with you," says the Lord. So, let us find joy on our way through the wilderness.

Amen.

# Emmanuel
Isaiah 7:10-16, Matthew 1:18-25

### Preached on December 22, 2019

WHAT WAS going on in Joseph's mind?

Can you imagine?

I know it's hard to imagine.

Joseph and Mary are saints of the Church and heroes of the faith. They are parents of the Christ child! It's hard to imagine them as having emotions or doubts like all the rest of us, but to fully grasp the magnitude of this second scripture lesson from the book of Matthew, it's important to recognize that Joseph and Mary were people.

Sometimes we think of the stories in Scripture as happening to spiritual figures who are somehow different from us. If we think that way, then we miss the point completely. So, imagine instead what you would be feeling if you were in Joseph's shoes.

Imagine that you're engaged to be married.

The wedding plans are in place.

There have already been multiple bridal showers.

Invitations have been sent.

Maybe, because you're a carpenter, you've already put an addition onto the house, or maybe you've been working on a bed for your bride to sleep in.

I don't know exactly what it was like. Neither does anyone else, so just imagine what it would have been like for you to find out that after you've told everyone and prepared in various ways that Mary was "found to be with child."

How would you have felt?

What would you have been thinking?

Now imagine what your mother would have said.

It's hard enough for the daughter- or son-in-law-to-be. I was once a son-in-law-to-be. I love my mother- and father-in-law very much. I've known them now for 20 years. For those 20 years, they have been as much a part of my life as my own parents. Their home, especially their vacation home on a mountain in North Carolina, feels like home to me. They've always welcomed me in and have been kind and loving beyond measure. But I will tell you this: About the time Sara and I were getting serious, her father bought a revolver.

He did.

He said it was because of the wild boar that had invaded their property up on the mountain. That's probably true, but by this purchase, it was clear to me that he had a gun, and he knew how to use it. And as I had been invited into the heart of his beloved daughter, I could imagine him using that gun for more than just protection from wild boar.

This is a precarious place, life as a son- or daughter-in-law-to-be.

I don't know whom my daughters are going to marry or fall in love with, but I already hate him or her. I do. And considering that hatred, I can imagine what was going on in the mind of Joseph's mother. I have an idea of what words of hers might have been poisoning her son's thoughts.

"Well, I never liked her anyway," his mother might have said.

"I told you to stay away from her," she might have added. "That's why I invited you to meet my friend Lois's daughter, Miriam. She's such a nice girl and she has class, unlike this Mary of yours."

This is part of the challenge of getting married: Your parents may have been looking for an opening to criticize your fiancé, and as soon as they have it, the flood gates open. That's not because they don't want you to be happy. It's because they love you and don't want you to get hurt.

I can just hear Joseph's father: "I knew that girl was going to break your heart, Joseph. But you weren't thinking, were you son?" Parents are like that. People are like that. We all are. We jump to conclusions. However, that's not just because we're prone to suspicion, conspiracy, or fear. We are prone to those things, of course. But we also jump to conclusions because we want to protect the ones we love from the ones who appear to be deceptive, dishonest, or disloyal.

The problem with such assumptions is that appearances can be deceiving.

You all know what they say about assumptions.

Have you ever thought about how many assumptions inform the opinions of your family members? Have you ever wondered whether or not those family members know how wrong the assumptions they are making are? Such would have been the case with Joseph's parents, his friends, and even Joseph himself, because Mary was found to be with child, but it's not what any of them thought. Still, I have to imagine that they were talking, and that Joseph was listening, because that's what people do. Therefore, "Her husband Joseph, being a righteous man and unwilling to expose her to public disgrace, planned to dismiss her quietly."

In those days he could have had her stoned, humiliated, or cast out from the community.

Because he was a kind man, he took all his assumptions and tempered them with compassion. Assuming he knew why she was with child, rather than give voice to his full anger or embarrassment, he was kind. I like that about him, but even his kindness was misinformed, for he was operating on the basis of assumption rather than truth.

That happens an awful lot.

Do you ever think about how much of our lives we spend misinformed?

Every morning, Thomas Jefferson woke up and placed his feet in a bucket of cold water because his doctors told him it was good for his health.

When George Washington was sick, the doctors rushed over and decided that his blood levels were out of whack, so they bled the poor man until he died.

Today there are people like me who will rub Bengay on any sore muscle, though its healing properties are unverified, and while its odor has proven to be highly offensive. Likewise, others will prescribe Robitussin for every malady. I'm always giving Becca Yan, a member of the church staff, a hard time for her conviction that essential oils will cure anything. (It sounds like witchcraft to me.)

Only who knows?

Who knows? We do. Or so we think.

Yet how often are our assumptions misleading us?

*Tied to What is Below*

How often do our prejudices misinform?

How many holiday dinners end with World War Three because Uncle Alfred is sure that his liberal grandchildren are communists, and his liberal grandchildren are sure that Uncle Alfred would vote for Atilla the Hun?

We don't really know, yet we think we do.

Our assumptions mislead us.

We take a few scattered observations and let them fill in the gaps.

Our minds run in circles based on misinformation.

I know it's hard to argue with the reality that this woman was with child, but let us all give thanks to God for Joseph, who was willing to abandon all of his assumptions in favor of a dream.

Now, be honest. You don't give much credence to dreams. Neither do I. But dreams do affect me. They affect Sara too. Some mornings Sara wakes up already mad at me, and for good reason. However, once or twice she woke up mad at me and I asked her what I had done. She looked at me and said, "Well, nothing I guess, but you won't believe what you did in my dreams last night!"

Has that ever happened to you?

Something like that happened to Joseph.

It was a dream, and it changed his world view. Only consider this: Mary was visited by an angel. All Joseph had to go on was a dream.

He could have explained that dream away saying, "It must have been indigestion."

He could have told his mother about it, and it wouldn't have stood up to all her assumptions.

He might have just allowed the dream to fuel his compassion, to affect his emotions but not his actions, and yet Joseph allowed this dream to change the course of his life and the fate of this world. It was a dream of the great promise made by God to humankind summed up in one word: Emmanuel.

That's a name, and it means simply: God with us.

God with us is very different from, "God looking down on us, trying to figure us out," or, "God making assumptions about who we are and what we're thinking." Emmanuel means, "God with us," knowing us, understanding us, in such a way that leaves no room for misinformation or assumptions.

That matters tremendously because in every human relationship. assumptions are being made. What we don't know, we often make up, and so often what we make up is worse than the truth. Consider *The Grinch*.

I've been under the weather, and so I've had a lot of time to watch my holiday movies. Maybe you haven't, so let me remind you. The Grinch lives in a cave on Mt. Crumpet. Mt. Crumpet looms over Whoville, and the Grinch lives in that cave with his dog Max. He thinks a lot about the Who's in Whoville, but he doesn't really know any of them well. He thinks he does, however. He assumes their Christmas is materialistic, that they don't care about people, unless those people are carrying toys. Only then he meets Cindy Lou Who. Cindy Lou Who is different. What does she want from Santa? Well, in the new Grinch movie, Cindy Lou Who only asks Santa that her Mom who works so hard would have a break.

The crucial plot twist of the movie is how she reacts when she wakes up on Christmas morning to find nothing under the tree. The Grinch assumed that Cindy Lou and every other Who in Whoville would be devastated when he stole all their Christmas stuff. He assumed that Christmas would be ruined! Instead, Cindy Lou and all the Who's in Whoville gather in the town square to sing that weird, nonsensical song, because Christmas in Whoville isn't about the stuff. The next twist is what happens when the Grinch hears them sing. Listening to their song he comes face to face with the truth. He learns who these Who's in Whoville really are. Then, his heart grows three sizes. Only, do you see what had to happen?

His assumptions had to die.

The distance between Mt. Crumpet and Whoville was bridged, not by what the Grinch thought he knew, but by the truth.

It was like a dream where he finally understood.

It was like a miracle when everything changed because he was close enough to really know. That's what Emmanuel means.

God comes to earth to become one of us, rather than rely on assumptions.

Can you imagine what would happen if our friends in Washington were so bold as to try and understand each other to such a degree? Can you imagine how dinner at Christmas would change if we were all so bold as to try and understand each other that way? In Christ, God has done it, for this is what love requires. More than that, in listening to each other, in striving to understand rather than assume we already know, we are continuing the work that our God has started in Emmanuel: God with us.

Amen.

# For A Child Has Been Born for Us
## Isaiah 9:2-7 and Luke 2:1-20

**Preached on December 24, 2019 - Christmas Eve.**

CHRISTMAS EVE is today, and Christmas Eve is a time for hospitality.

We set big dining room tables and make room by the fire.

Those guest rooms that most of the time are turned into laundry rooms are made guest rooms again so family or friends have a place to lay their heads.

This is a time for joining together and carol-singing. I'm willing to bet that even those of you who have a designated pew in here where you always sit have made room for those who are joining us for the first time.

All of that is good, because being left out hurts.

I remember being in middle school and finding out about this boy/girl party. It was one of the first boy/girl parties I remember. I think I remember it so well because I wasn't invited.

Do you know that feeling?

Whether it's large or small, that feeling of rejection is one you never forget, but in this world of ours not everyone can be invited to everything, even on Christmas Eve.

There's limited seating, so it always seems, or maybe we could do a better job of making room.

I remember well my grandfather telling me about big meals his mother would cook out in the country where they lived. He grew up in a place called the Caw-Caw Swamp. His father was the game warden, and often men would come around to lend a hand. These men were unrefined, as men in the Caw-Caw Swamp tended to be, but as a son to the game warden, my grandfather enjoyed a level of gentility. His family had a radio, and one Christmas, a man who had come to lend a hand heard a fine violinist play over the radio. This Caw-Caw swamp native stopped to listen and then declared: "It sounds like he's got a pretty good fiddle, if only he knew how to play it right."

That's a good story. A funny one. Another story that I remember which isn't so funny is that my grandfather told me any hired hands who were white took their meals in the kitchen of that house. Those who were Black took their meals on the back steps, because not everyone was invited in.

So, it was with Mary.

So, it was with Joseph.

When it came to them, that Christmas Eve so long ago, it probably wasn't because of the color of their skin that they were left out. But just the same, they had no room of their own at the inn. They were left out.

They had traveled so far just to be sent out back to the manger.

Still, they made the best of it. "She gave birth to her firstborn son and wrapped him in bands of cloth and laid him in a manger."

Now having a new baby changes things.

I can imagine that suddenly these who were left out of the inn are now in the position of deciding who gets to see the baby, and everyone wants to see a baby. I can imagine ladies who worked at the inn gathering around Mary. Maybe the inn keeper's daughter peeked in to see who was making all the noise. Maybe the inn keeper, herself, wanted to come down with her husband to see the baby.

Had I been Joseph, I would have turned them both around.

In fact, when Sara and I were new parents, we turned a lot of people around. Even those who were allowed inside were subjected to scrutiny. We made them sanitize their hands. Anyone under the weather was subject to a health screening. No one was allowed to touch the baby's face or hands. We even bought these medical shoe covers that we made people put over their shoes before coming in to keep them from tracking in outside contaminants.

That's just how some new parents are.

They act like they're the first people to have ever done it.

Boldly, we were guarding the door even to those who came bearing gifts. We subjected them all to scrutiny and put out a genuine spirit of inhospitality, because new parents are in the position of deciding who is allowed in and who is left out.

What about Mary?

What about Joseph?

How did they do it? Who did they leave out?

*"In that region there were shepherds living in the fields, keeping watch over their flocks by night. An angel of the Lord stood before them, and the glory of the Lord shone around them, and they were terrified. But the angel said to them, "Do not be afraid; for see – I am bringing you good news of great joy for all the people: to you is born this day in the city of David a Savior, who is the Messiah, the Lord.*

*When the angels had left them and gone into heaven, the shepherds said to one another, "Let us go now to Bethlehem and see this thing that has taken place. So, they went with haste and found Mary and Joseph, and the child lying in the manger."*

But Joseph said to the shepherds, "Wait just a minute. First, I'm going to need you to put these cover things over your shoes. I don't want you tracking any germs in here."

No, that's not what happened. You know what happened, only have you ever really thought about it?

From the very beginning, it's all right there.

Before he could say his first word, already, the one who was left out of the inn welcomes all people to himself.

In his moment of rejection, still he turns the other cheek.

Rather than return evil for evil, though he is the stone that the builders rejected, he is the chief cornerstone of a new kingdom where all people, no matter how lowly, have a seat at the table and are welcomed inside.

That's Jesus.

That's the little child lying in a manger - God incarnate.

He is true God from true God, shining the bright light on the truth, that no matter how rejected you have ever felt in your life, the Christ child welcomes you in.

Don't you see?

From the very beginning he knew that feeling of being left out, set aside, and looked over. Yet in his very birth he challenges any idea of limited space at the table by inviting the shepherds in.

That's a radical message of hospitality that challenges a core fear that rots the heart of our society.

That's a radical message of inclusion that even challenges some core declarations made by the church.

The great sign of the shepherds who were invited to his manger bed is that there is more room, more grace, more love, more forgiveness, and more freedom than we had dared to believe.

We turn our backs, while the Christ child calls them closer saying, "I was born for you."

We close our doors, while the Christ child invites them in.

We build walls and fences, though he cries out to the entire world, just as he calls out to you and me. And that's not theoretical. That's literal.

You. I'm looking right at you. You. He was born for you.

Hear the truth of that.

"To you is born this day in the city of David, a Savior, who is the Messiah the Lord," and that's regardless of how unworthy you feel, but what it demands is that you look upon other people the same way that God looks upon you.

The whole world would change with just this simple recognition, for while our society is divided between those who have and those who have not, those who live in gated communities and those who live on the south side of fences, those who have papers and those who don't have them, those who were accepted and those who weren't accepted, those who went to cotillion and those who use the wrong fork at the dinner table, at the Lord's table there is no partiality, so how can there be any in our hearts?

Christmas Eve is a time for hospitality. That's because He was born for each and every one of you and each and every one of them, so make some room.

That's the change that's required of all of us who celebrate the birth of this homeless, migrant child. Born of Mary, son of God, unto you and unto me.

Alleluia, and Amen.

# Called but not Qualified
## Isaiah 42:1-9 and Matthew 3:13-17

### Preached on January 12, 2020

LAST THURSDAY was a special night for me. Having been nominated by Jim Kerr, I was honored to be named among the top twenty under 40 in Cobb County. They gave me a fancy glass trophy and had me walk across the stage, while several members of our congregation who were in attendance cheered, which made me feel very special. But as the other names were called and all their accomplishments were listed, I started to feel a little out of place.

At the end of the ceremony, before cocktails on the roof of the Strand Theater, I bumped into Trevor Beemon, Executive Director of Cobb Landmarks and the William Root House and also one of the 20 under 40. We agreed that we both felt like imposters. "I mean, a guy who was on TV on The Voice was up there," he said, noting that we had been grouped with truly incredible people.

Later, I ran into that guy who was on The Voice in the stairwell. I told him I was honored to be included in this group with him, and he said, "Oh man. I felt so out of place. I had to go up on the stage right after that lady who is the south east's top building contractor, who also happens to be a helicopter commander. I'm just a singer!"

That made me feel better, because I guess we all feel unworthy at times.

Look at John the Baptist.

Our second scripture lesson begins:

*"Then Jesus came from Galilee to John at the Jordan, to be baptized by him. John would have prevented him, saying, 'I need to be baptized by you, and do you come to me?'"*

The author of the book of Matthew tells us that John would have prevented him. I can understand that because getting called on by God to do something so incredible is a terrifying thing. Being called on by God to do anything important is terrifying, because it makes us all, even John the Baptist, feel unworthy.

I'll never forget how our neighbor back in Tennessee, a great Episcopalian named Kile Patrick, called his wife Connie just to say, "I just had the most incredible thought. If my cell phone rang and the caller ID said that it was God calling, would I pick up?"

Not everybody would.

Not everybody does.

Think about it.

Isn't it an overwhelming thought that God would call on you or me to do something for him? So, just about every time it happens. the one who's called on hesitates.

The Lord appeared to Moses in the Burning Bush and Moses says, "Who am I that I should go to Pharaoh."

The Lord called on the young Jeremiah and he says, "Wait a minute. I am only a boy."

The Lord calls Isaiah and Isaiah says, "Woe is me! I am lost, for I am a man of unclean lips, and I live among a people of unclean lips."

The phone rings and God is calling, but not many people are ready to pick it up. So also, Jesus came to John at the Jordan to be baptized by him, and John would have prevented him asking, "Who am I to be baptized by you?"

Isn't that what we all ask?

Who am I to serve the church as an Elder?

Who am I to be a Deacon?

Who am I to teach?

Who am I to comfort those who mourn?

Who am I to preach?

How do any of us respond to the honor of being called? And yet, we must play our part, for Christianity is not a spectator sport, though sometimes we treat it like it is. Sometimes we walk into this sanctuary, and because there are seats out there and there's a platform up here, it's easy to fall into the misconception that this place is something like a theater. In a theater, there are three basic stations and three basic roles. There's the audience, the actors on the stage and then there's the director who is back behind the curtain. That's true in so many places we go. At a dance recital, there are the dancers on the stage, the instructors are behind the curtain helping them along, and the parents and grandparents are loving every minute of it in the audience.

But this sanctuary is different.

Every church is different, because when we are bold to see God at work and when we are courageous enough to answer the call, the whole world is different. According to the great Danish philosopher Soren Kierkegaard, in the sanctuary God is the audience, you are the ones on stage, and it is the job of those of us who stand up here to direct you in your performance of praise and worship.

How, then, is it if someone falls asleep in the back?

To God, it is the same as if a dancer fell asleep on stage.

Christianity, like life, is not a spectator sport, though some treat it as though it were. Some are called on, but don't pick up the phone. They don't feel worthy, able, or as though they have the time. However, the Lord calls on humans to take on divine work, just as Jesus called on John at the Jordan.

John doesn't feel worthy to do so.

Neither do I.

We sing to worship God in here, but why would God want to hear us sing? It sounds strange that God would need our voices, maybe because we don't know that God uses them, but let me tell you something, God does. I was at a funeral last Thursday. Many of you were there too. Our choir sang. At the reception, Mayor Tumlin walked up to me and he said, "That choir is amazing. And to think that all those people would show up to sing on a Thursday at 2:00."

Why did they do that?

Maybe some of them asked themselves the same question: "Why should I show up to sing when there is work to do, and laundry to fold, and what difference will it make any way?" These are the questions that we ask, while God calls us to lift up our voices because it is the music which points to the truth that we cannot comprehend. It is the choir who lifts up the faint-hearted, for the presence of mere mortals brings comfort to the broken hearted.

Do you know that?

It's true.

God calls us and uses us, but like John, we hesitate, saying, "I'm not worthy." Take heart, then, because God doesn't call perfect people. God doesn't call the qualified. God qualifies the called. Christianity, like life, is no spectator sport, and just as Jesus called on John to baptize him in the Jordan, so also you and I are called on every single time a baby is baptized here.

You are not to watch as I sprinkle that water on her head, but to participate, making promises to everyone who is baptized here "to receive the child into the life of the church" and to "support and encourage her through prayer and example to be faithful in Christian Discipleship."

You and I have been called because we have a job to do.

Now that I've explained baptism this way you might be thinking what John was thinking and wishing that you hadn't made the promises that you made. But hear what Jesus said to John. "Let it be so now; for it is proper for us in this way to fulfill all righteousness."

Isn't it a miracle, an amazing miracle, that all righteousness is fulfilled with the help of a human's hands? Isn't it a miracle that a church is called on to teach a child about the grace of God?

This is God's way: the divine inviting the human, not to stand by and watch, but to play a part. Consider for just a moment how many human beings played their part in loving you so that you became the person you are today. I was standing there with Mayor Tumlin as he was celebrating our choir. Then he noticed Victoria Chastain, our former mayor, standing there handing out glasses of water. "Is that the kind of job I have to look forward to as an ex-mayor of the city of Marietta?" he asked. They both laughed and across the room a woman looked at me and walked over.

She looked me in the eye and said, "Do you remember who I am?"

I said, "Of course I can. You're Mrs. Peterson! My teacher!"

She said, "Well, yes, but it's Mrs. Pickett."

Then I said, "Of course, Mrs. Pickett, my third-grade teacher."

She said, "Well, it was fifth grade, but yes."

We talked for a while, and she told me she wished she could go dig up some of the things I wrote when I was in her class at Hickory Hills Elementary school, and the thing I wanted to say, but couldn't, is that she loved how I wrote and I remember. She bound up our writing in little books, and she asked me to read mine to the whole school at an assembly. My book was called the Swamp Monster, and she loved it. It made me feel so good that my teacher loved it. My parents meant to be there when I read it to the school, but they got mixed up about the time, so when I cried because they weren't there, Mrs. Pickett gave me a hug and it meant the whole world.

Or it might have been my third-grade teacher, Mrs. Peterson. Regardless, my point is this: There are people who made all the difference to me. Some of them are here right now, because God uses mortals to participate in the divine story that is changing us and the world.

Jesus called on John to baptize him in the Jordan, just as he calls on you, and just as he calls on me.

We may not be qualified, but we are called, so say yes.

Amen.

# Getting Out of the Way
## Isaiah 49:1-7 and John 1:29-42

### Preached on January 19, 2020

LAST THURSDAY afternoon I saw something remarkable. Remarkable things happen all the time and I'm thankful when I notice them. Our daughter, Lily, was the one who pointed this one out. We were walking with her friend Julia, leaving the church after helping out at Club 3:30, our afterschool program. Once she pointed it out, we all stopped dead in our tracks because walking across the Harris Hines Memorial Bridge was a pink dog.

That's right. A pink dog.

The woman walking the dog saw us gawking, but just kept strolling normally, as though she were walking a normal dog. She wasn't. That dog was pink, and we caught up to her to ask her about it. Once we caught up, we found that this pink dog belongs to Maggie, daughter of Janet Lewis. Maggie just wanted to give her dog a pink mohawk, only the dog moved while she was dyeing it, so Maggie ended up dyeing her whole dog pink, which is something that never once occurred to me to do.

I've never thought of dyeing my dog's hair, but Maggie has.

Isn't that remarkable?

It's so important to stop and notice when you see something remarkable. The most remarkable sight that anyone has ever seen walked up to John the Baptist and John the Baptist stopped to notice.

Last Sunday we focused on John the Baptist, just as we do today, but this week is different. Last week we read a Scripture lesson from the Gospel of Matthew that described John's willingness to step forward to baptize Jesus. In that instance, John hesitated, not feeling worthy of baptizing Jesus. However, in stepping forward and answering the call to baptize the Lord in the Jordan, John models a courage that we need to have, for God also calls on us all to step forward. On the other hand, while John the Baptist had the courage to step forward even though he felt unworthy, what we see in today's scripture lesson from the Gospel of John is that he also had the wisdom to step back in awe and wonder.

Last week he stepped forward to do something.

This week he gets out of the way.

We must be able to do both, possessing the wisdom to know which we should do at any given time. Not everyone has that kind of wisdom, but people must know how to step back. If they don't, they can be very annoying to be around.

There are some people in this world who don't know when to step forward to speak, but at the same time there are plenty of people who don't know when to stop talking.

There are some people in this world who never try, but there are plenty of other people who try too hard.

There are some people in this world who don't know how to accept praise and have no capacity to receive a compliment, but there are so many others who never step back to give others their due, serving as the president of their own fan club, wanting all the good news to be about them. Do you know anyone like that?

I feel sure that you do, because while there are people who have trouble stepping forward, there are others who don't know how to step back, so consider John again today. Last Sunday we saw how he stepped up to ministry when he was called on. Today we see that he also steps back for when he saw Jesus coming toward him, he points away from himself to declare, "Here is the Lamb of God who takes away the sin of the world!"

In thinking about John's example now for two weeks in a row, I realize that I don't always have the courage or the nerve to step forward. Neither do I always have the wisdom or humility to step back.

A funny thing about being a preacher is that you stand at the door as everyone leaves the service. The reason we do this is to greet you, the members of the congregation, and to connect with you as your pastors. An added bonus is that we also become those who receive all the compliments. You are such a gracious group of people, and you so generously tell me when the choir sang so beautifully, when the flowers looked just perfect, even when the floors are clean. Regardless of whom should receive the compliment I am often the one who receives them.

Do you know what I always say? "Thank you."

I guess there's nothing else I could say. Only consider for a moment just how many hands go into crafting this worship service. Someone must print the bulletins; another must hand them out. There are speakers and microphones which have been maintained and controlled from up in the sound booth. Music is played on the organ, prayers have been written and proofread, and hymns are sung. There are too many parts of this worship service for any one person to take credit for. Plus, all of what goes on here is empty without the Holy Spirit, yet I am the one who says, "Thank you." That doesn't make any sense; however, this is so often the way it is.

Consider all the people you know who never step back to thank those whose shoulders they stand on.

How many quarterbacks bask in the limelight without thanking those who blocked for them? How many dig into their meal without giving thanks to God from whom all blessings flow and for the hands who prepared the food?

How many hours in a day do we spend looking at our phones when pink dogs are walking by? We wake up to scarlet sunrises.

We sleep under a galaxy of stars.

Even still, some spend so much time navel gazing that they would have failed to take notice of even "the lamb of God who takes away the sins of the world."

I'm as guilty as anybody. The church I served in Lilburn was facing a financial crisis, which they emerged from. They went from a massive forecasted budget deficit to a large financial surplus. When I left that church for First Presbyterian Church in Columbia, TN, a former college president, Dr. Herold Pryor had heard this story from my resume. At a meet-and-greet with the entire congregation present, he asked me down in the Fellowship Hall what I had done to achieve such a success. Sarcastically I said, "Well, I'm a financial genius."

Of course, that isn't true.

I'm not a financial genius.

Still, it was on my resume because it's hard to explain when the God of miracles acts and it's easy for humans to take the credit.

We all want to be the somebody who can fix it or did fix it.

We see problems and we pressure leaders to do something about them.

If a leader of this country were to say, "Well, I've prayed about unemployment and I trust that God will do something about it," she'd never get elected because it seems passive to step back and point to the heavens. No one wants to admit that they can't do it, nor do they want to admit that they can't help for we're all the time pretending we have it all together. Therefore, it's time we learned from John that having it all together is not what's required.

I think about the Rev. Billy Graham. You know he preached across the country and the world, asking us to do this one thing: "Will you accept Jesus Christ as your Lord and Savior?" Who knows how many lives he changed just by asking this one question? Who knows how many faced their end without fear because of their answer? But we must not think for a minute that this is a simple request, for acknowledging Christ as Lord and Savior requires accepting that we cannot save ourselves.

That's a hard thing to do.

Don't think it's not, for we all fall into the trap of believing that we're doing pretty well on our own, that we just need to work a little bit harder or that we can hold it all together if we just wake up a little earlier.

That's how many of us are, so listen to this: Someone once asked Billy Graham's wife, Ruth, who was a Presbyterian, if she'd ever considered divorce. She said, "Oh no. Absolutely not. However, I've often considered murder."

That's a funny story, but I tell it because it's also a liberating one.

Don't look to the mere mortal.

Look to the one all the great preachers, mere mortals themselves, have pointed towards, because everyone is in need of His grace. Everyone.

That Prayer of Confession in your bulletin: do you know who it comes from? Me. Do you know where I gain inspiration for those prayer? My sin. So maybe some of these prayers don't all fit your life, but don't go through that thing like a checklist. Because these are my confessions, I worry that they don't always fit your life, only don't look at that prayer and think through it like this way:

Together we prayed, "We confess that we have not sought your face," but I worry that someone might have added to their prayer, "Well God, maybe Joe hasn't, but I've been seeking your face." Then we continued, "Focused on ourselves we look past your presence and the needs of others," and maybe someone looked heavenward, self-satisfied, saying, "All good there." Then finally the prayer continued, "Rather than sing the praise of our redeemer, we take center stage." Did any of you pray, "Lord, I'm good here too, but we have some work to do on our preacher"?

Some of us read through the prayer of confession on Sunday morning and use it as a nice, weekly, internal audit. Only that's not the point, because while we all want to be good, while we all want to be innocent, the Prayer of Confession invites us to face our faults so that we can receive His grace.

That's the truth.

I know doing so is a lot to ask.

We don't want to ask for help.

No one does.

No one likes the truth that we are broken and need God's healing. We like to teach and don't want to be taught. Knowing how stubborn we can all be, recognize the strength it took for John the Baptist who "saw Jesus coming toward him and declared, 'Here is the Lamb of God who takes away the sin of the world!'"

He was bold to say, "It's not me. It's him. I can't do it, but he can. I cannot hold it together, and here is one who holds the whole world in his hands. I am not good, but he is so good."

A counselor once said it to me this way: sometimes we must stop trying to fill our own cup, to see that he has already filled it. We must step back from our problems to see him answer our prayers. We struggle to be worthy because we want to be loved. But step back, because you are already. Get out of the way and allow him to do for you what you cannot do for yourself.

Amen.

# Leaving Father Zebedee
Isaiah 9:1-4 and Matthew 4:12-23

### Preached on January 26, 2020

THERE ARE several good questions to ask when you first read this second scripture lesson from the Gospel of Matthew. I think the first one that I ask is, "What was it about Jesus?"

These four fishermen just stopped and followed.

How did they know it was him?

How did they know Jesus was someone who was worth following?

There are some good explanations. We're not unfamiliar with the leadership quality called "command presence." Command presence is this quality that's not easy to define, exactly. It's one of those "you know it when you see it" things. Looking back at history, we know George Washington must have had it. As a man over six feet tall in the late 18th century he was always the tallest man in the room. He was known to be the best horsemen as well, and when he barked an order, most people fell in line. He had command presence.

The same could be said of others like General Patton, Dr. Martin Luther King, Jr., Dr. Jim Speed, or my wife Sara Evans.

What was it about Jesus?

Was he tall?

Was he commanding?

Could he persuade a crowd with the truth of his words and the sound of his voice?

Dr. Roger Nishioka thinks that it's something more than that when it comes to Jesus. Roger was a professor at Columbia Theological Seminary while I was there. He's a big name in the Presbyterian Church, and in a commentary on this passage, Dr. Nishioka quoted his father, who said, "We are imprinted with a memory of God, and God is imprinted with a memory of us, and even if it takes a lifetime, we will find each other."

What was it, then, about Jesus?

According to Nishioka, it is like those newborn baby seals numbering in the hundreds or the thousands on a single beach. These beaches are packed with all these baby seals who all look alike, but as their mothers return from the ocean with their catch, the pups find the mothers or the mothers find their pups because from the moment of birth, "the sound and scent of the pup are imprinted in the mother's memory, and the sound and scent of the mother are imprinted in the pup's."

Could it be then that even before we are born, we are imprinted with the memory of God, so that when we hear His voice, we just know to follow? I think that must be how it is, and so St. Augustine was so bold to write at the beginning of his Confession that:

*Man is one of your creatures, Lord, and his instinct is to praise you. The thought of you stirs him so deeply that he cannot be content unless he praises you, because you made us for yourself and our hearts find no peace until they rest in you.*

For him, even while his childhood and young adulthood were spent wandering so far that he was at first rendered ineligible for baptism, for they said, "He was a great sinner for so small a boy," still Augustine found no satisfaction in the pleasures of the world. He only found peace by resting in the Lord, for when we hear His voice we hear the call of home.

Or, to put it as GK Chesterton does in his great poem of Christ's birth in the manger:

*There fared a mother driven forth*
*Out of an inn to roam;*
*In the place where she was homeless*
*All men are at home.*
*For men are homesick in their homes,*
*And strangers under the sun,*
*And they lay their heads in a foreign land*
*Whenever the day is done.*
*To an open house in the evening*
*Home shall men come,*
*To an older place than Eden*
*And a taller town than Rome.*
*To the end of the way of the wandering star,*
*To the things that cannot be and that are,*
*To the place where God was homeless*
*And all men are at home.*

What, then, did these fishermen see in Jesus as he wandered up the beach? What did they sense in His demeanor? What did they hear in His voice? They heard a voice they had always known but couldn't place and they saw a man they recognized but whose name they could not remember. They had always known Him, and yet they hadn't met, and they knew to follow though they could not have told you why.

The words of the Prophet Isaiah that made up our 1st scripture lesson is quoted again in the 2nd, claiming that seeing Him is as "the people who sat in darkness" seeing a great light, that on "those who sat in the region and shadow of death light has dawned."

That was Jesus. When you've seen him and when you've heard him, you just know.

Meeting him is like looking into the eyes of your newborn child. She's breathing her first breaths and yet you recognize her face somehow. You don't need explanation, for the truth isn't so hard to recognize when you hear it. It's like water to the thirsty. It's like water to the thirsty who didn't even know that they were thirsty, for in Him is the satisfaction for our deepest need. "Bind our wandering hearts to thee," we sing, because our hearts find no rest until they rest in him. We are "imprinted with a memory of God, and God is imprinted with a memory of us," and even if it takes a lifetime, we will find each other and when we do we will finally be at home.

He found those four and they followed.

Perhaps this is where there is sometimes a difference between them and us.

I want to argue that we would have known it was Jesus as they did, because the imprint of our creator is inside us just as it was inside them. We know Jesus's voice when we hear it, but the question is: Would we have followed?

It's not whether we would have recognized him. You would have and so would I, but would we have followed?

Think for a moment about what these fishermen had to leave behind.

In becoming his first disciples, what were they willing to give up?

Verse 18 says it all:

*As he walked by the Sea of Galilee, he saw two brothers, Simon, who is called Peter, and Andrew his brother, casting a net into the sea for they were fishermen. And he said to them,*

*"Follow me, and I will make you fish for people." Immediately they left their nets and followed him. As he went from there, he saw two other brothers, James son of Zebedee and his brother John, in the boat with their father Zebedee, mending their nets, and he called them. Immediately they left the boat and their father and followed him.*

What were they willing to give up?

What did they leave behind?

They left behind their nets, livelihood, and all that they had known.

They left behind their trade, heritage, people, home, family, and poor old father Zebedee is left in that boat.

I say that when you hear the voice of God you know it, but are we able to get up and follow? That's a big part of the challenge of being a Christian today. Preachers like me make it too easy. Someone will ask me what the requirements of church membership are. When I hear that question, I'm just so glad they're interested, I don't ask them to do a thing. Just join the church, please!

However, here's the truth: If you want a new life in Christ, you must leave the old life behind.

In Chapter 10 of Matthew, Jesus says it himself, "Those who find their life will lose it, and those who lose their life for my sake will find it." What, then, is the cost of discipleship? What do you have to give up to really follow him?

Back in Tennessee, in an African Methodist Episcopal Church we sang about it once. The Presbyterian Church I served there started a relationship with Bethel Chapel AME and for our third joint worship service, the service began with a song that was easy to learn but profound in its message. It went like this:

*Victory is mine*
*Victory is mine*
*Victory today is mine.*
*I'll tell Satan*
*Get thee behind*
*Victory today is mine.*

We sang that until we got it. It took the Presbyterians a little while, but we got it. When we did the Music Director at Bethel Chapel AME changed the words a little bit and we sang:

*Happiness is mine*
*Happiness is mine*
*Happiness today is mine*

The part of this hymn which struck me so profoundly is the claim within it, that for happiness to be mine I must tell Satan to "get thee behind". I hear in these words the cost of discipleship. That is, in order to inherit the gifts of God, have the joy He intends and follow where He leads, I must leave my net, old life, and maybe even my father behind, because even the people we love can hold us back from enjoying the majesty of new life. Likewise, what becomes clear from this passage from the Gospel of Matthew is that recognizing Jesus is one thing but leaving behind what must be left behind is another. Perhaps, when you consider how clear Jesus is about the cost and how upfront this scripture lesson is about what must be left behind, you'll see that those who are worth following never gloss over the fine print.

You remember well the words: "It's not what this country can do for you, it's what you can do for this country." This well-phrased line from a great president makes it clear that there's a cost.

"Cheap grace is the preaching of forgiveness without requiring repentance, baptism without church discipline. Communion without confession. Cheap grace is grace without discipleship, grace without the cross, grace without Jesus Christ." That's a quote from Dietrich Bonhoeffer. He died in a Nazi Concentration Camp. Why did he die there, though he was not a Jew? It's because he was a follower of Jesus in a time of tyranny and following Jesus is risky.

On the other hand, going along with the crowd is not discipleship.

Falling in line with the powers that be is not the same as obedience to the Gospel.

The cost is made clear when you consider how Christ was tried, condemned, and crucified by those who would rather maintain their power than hear the truth.

This religion of ours is clear about the cost.

Joy is the Father's intention, but to have it, some things must be left behind.

What have you been asked to leave behind?

Is it your net or your father?

Is it a bad habit or an old dream?

Is it hatred, hypocrisy, appearances, ego, or public opinion?

Whatever it is and no matter how hard it is to let go, know this: "This present time [is] not worth comparing with the glory about to be revealed to us." So, do not cling too tightly to the present or to what you have, for we have been called by the Savior to something better. Go tell Satan, "get thee behind" for I have heard his voice and I want to follow where he leads.

Amen.

# Choose Life
Deuteronomy 30:15-20 and Matthew 5:21-37

### **Preached on February 16, 2020**

SCRIPTURE IS easy to misunderstand.

I don't understand a lot of the Bible. There are parts that I do understand, other parts that I'm trying to understand, but there are many who misunderstand most of it and that's probably because misunderstanding the Bible is easy to do.

It might be easier to misunderstand than the Bible than it is to understand it. That's how it is with people, so why would it not also be the case that Scripture is also more than meets the eye? When we encounter strong moral admonitions like that of the two Scripture lessons we've just read, it's possible to misunderstand the intention of our God just as children misunderstand the intentions of their parents on earth.

I wonder if it has ever been the case with you parents, that when attempting to save your children from harm, self-inflicted or otherwise, they've reacted as though you were not trying to save them at all, but instead, as though you were trying to ruin their lives.

Last Sunday afternoon we were on the way to the Cub Scout Troop 252 Blue and Gold Banquet. That's an annual event for our Scout troop which celebrates the birth of scouting. Because our scout troop, like many others, has gone co-ed, our 8-year-old daughter, Cece, has joined the troop that both my brother and I were in, and which my father, Cece's grandfather, served as a leader. I took both girls to the Blue and Gold Banquet along with our covered dish. On the way there, coming out of the house they beat me to the car. Locking the door to the house, then walking towards the car, I could see that Lily, who is now old enough to sit in the front seat, was there in the front seat, already buckled. When I opened the door, I found Cece, though only 8-years-old, in the driver's seat. I couldn't see her until I opened the door because she was lying down so that her feet could reach the pedals. From that position she said, "Daddy, I'm tall enough to reach the peddles. Why don't you let me drive us to the church?"

That's a fair question.

I responded with a couple fair answers:

1. Because you don't know how to drive.

2. Because if you're lying down in the driver's seat to touch the pedals, you can't see over the steering wheel.

3. Because you don't have a driver's license, and so it's illegal for you to drive the car.

These are only three of the logical reasons why I couldn't allow Cece to drive us to the Blue and Gold Banquet. A more emotional one: Because I love you and don't want you to wreck this car and get hurt. Regardless, my logic was met with complete and utter indignation by both of them. Our children reacted to me as though I had suddenly mandated that no children in the Evans household be allowed to eat, smile, or drink water again. Though I was standing on the moral high ground they lashed out at me, saying: "Gosh Dad! You never let us do anything!"

Consider that experience and reflect for a moment on your relationship with God.

Or think for a moment about someone else's relationship with God.

It is a common thing to begin our prayers, "Our Father," and so also, it is a common thing for us and many others to encounter God's law with the same indignation as children to their parents. "Why should I let God tell me what to do?" some ask, as though the God's intention is to keep us from happiness or fun, rather than ensure that we enjoy the benefits of an abundant life. Too many have rejected the Church because they believe that a life of fulfilment will be found outside of it, and too many inside the Church validate such an assumption by living miserable lives that no sane person would ever want to imitate.

Jesus commands that we be salt and light. I remember talking with my barber about the passage as few years ago. He told me that salt is good, so we need to be salt. "Without it, food tastes boring, and I sure have been to some boring churches."

Why would Jesus tell us to be salt?

Why would Moses tell us that in God's law is life?

Then, considering today's second scripture lesson from the Gospel of Matthew, why would Jesus call us to watch not just our actions, but our thoughts? Some say it's because God doesn't want us to have any fun, but I say it's because God wants us to choose life and not death.

The Choir just sang so beautifully: "If you love him, keep his commandments," but don't forget, it's because God loves us that God gave them. God's intention in giving us rules to live by is not to rain on our parade, but to ensure that we avoid hurting ourselves and the people around us. God gives commands for the same reason that loving parents stop their 8-year-olds from driving the car. It is for love that God does it.

Still, so many, when reading a list of moral admonitions like the ones we've just read from the Gospel of Matthew, would say, "Why follow those rules? I'd rather live a little!"

Live a little?

Some say such things as though a life of sin were a life of freedom.

Does a life of indulging the flesh lead to fulfillment?

Does breaking the rules ensure happiness?

To quote the worst hymn to sing but my favorite one to quote:

*We are not free when we're confined*

*to every wish that sweeps the mind,*

*but free when freely we accept*

*the sacred bounds that must be kept.*

And what are those sacred bounds? We just read them. These moral admonitions from the very mouth of our Lord do not abolish the law but fulfill it. God's word for us today is one that requires self-examination, change, and repentance, for Christ does not just call us to refrain from murder, but even the thought of it!

It's true.

Is there forgiveness in our Lord? Of course.

Is there love? Absolutely.

In God is all compassion and goodness, for God is one who loves us too much to allow us to stay as we are. As God opens the car door of our inner thoughts to see us trying to drive without seeing over the steering wheel of our lives, God says simply, "Get out of the front seat and listen to what I have to say."

"Your thoughts are dangerous," God says.

That's the point of this entire second scripture lesson. When we really think about it, we know God is right. Our thoughts are dangerous.

I've been using an app on my phone to meditate every morning. In addition to reading a short devotional, then praying through my personal list and the list that Rev. Joe Brice provides, I use this guided meditation app to spend time in the presence of God in quiet, for so often my prayers are too much talking and not enough listening. The guided meditation suggested that I notice my thoughts, then label them - that I think about what I'm thinking about. That's a strange concept, but it's helped me. If I'm at home and my mind has wandered, just noticing what that thought was about tells me something. So, I ask myself, was that thought about my children, my wife, my parents, or much more likely, work?

In labeling my thoughts I begin to notice where my mind is, for my mind is not always in the same place as my body, nor are my thoughts always bringing me closer to the people right beside me. I was thinking about changing the title to this sermon to more accurately reflect what I'm trying to say this morning, and so I came up with the alternative title: "Your Phone Is from the Devil."

I don't really think that. Not exactly, anyway.

Your phone, like so many other things - money, guns, anger, sex - can be used for good or for evil, depending on how you use it. The intention, of course, is to provide connection, and indeed it does. Because of technology and the power of the internet, our worship service reaches all the way to our friend Kay and her family in Australia. But sitting next to my wife on the couch, my phone can also take me right back to my office at the church. It can distract me from my family. With Facebook, where bridges are burnt between me and all my Facebook friends once I learn how they really think, it can threaten my most important relationships because my phone can take me anywhere and it can show me anything.

Be careful with that thing.

Why?

Because if you're mad at someone you need to go and tell them why your mad, you don't need to vent on Facebook. God created us to love and put us in relationships. God gave us feelings of attraction, sexual and otherwise, and if you get used to watching other people through pornography you won't be able to do it right with the person who you're supposed to be doing it with.

What did Jesus say? He quoted Moses and the Law.

Moses said, "You shall not murder." Good. Don't. But don't think about murdering people all day either because hate will rot you out from the inside.

Moses said, "Don't commit adultery," and he was right. Don't. But thinking about adultery all day is going to mess you up too.

Then, on divorce - "Whoever divorces his wife, let him give her a certificate of divorce.'" OK, but if you think you can end a relationship with a piece of paper then you're crazy, because the hate you feel towards him or the resentment you feel towards her will still hurt your kids even after the separation. They can feel it. Watch your thoughts.

But have you ever been afraid that God was watching them? I have. And whether you think of God as a loving parent or a judgmental one matters tremendously in this way, because whether God wants to help us change so that we'd have joy, or wants to see our thoughts so that God can judge us and reject us makes all the difference in the world.

Know this, then: Jesus isn't talking about thoughts because he's a member of the thought police. Jesus isn't calling us to look inside our heads, so we'll be consumed by guilt or shame. Jesus doesn't call us to monitor what we're thinking so we'll know whether we are among the righteous or the unrighteous. Instead, God gives us these instructions because the choice is always ours: abundant life or death. And like Moses, God calls us to choose life.

Stop worrying about what other people are doing and recognize where your thoughts are leading you. Just stop. That's what this is about. Just stop hating, lusting, gossiping, coveting, and being jealous, and live.

So often our society points fingers at the ones who dance during the Super Bowl. Don't worry about how they dance or what they wear. They can't hurt you. Worry about the thoughts in your head, because they can hurt you. It's time to stop worrying about who can go in which bathroom and what happens in other people's bedrooms, because Christ calls us to consider what happens in our own bathrooms, our own bedrooms, and in between our own ears.

Everyone knows that the grown-ups in Washington can't get along, but don't worry so much about it that you fail to worry about how what you say about them is affecting your relationship with your friends and your family. What matters so much to Jesus here is how we get along with the people we actually know, not how we view the people we see on TV.

"I say to you that if you are angry with a brother or sister, you will be liable to judgement… So, when you are offering your gift at the altar, if you remember that your brother or sister has something against you, leave your gift and go; be reconciled [!]" And if you do, you will live. Choose life.

Amen.

# Part 3 - From the Mountain Top to the Quarantine

THIS BLOCK of sermons, which begins on Transfiguration Sunday, spans the Lenten Season of 2019. By this point in the year, news of COVID-19 was spreading even more quickly than the virus. Transfiguration Sunday is a celebration of the love which transformed Jesus, and a call to honor the same kind of transformation which love always requires. This virus demanded that we change so much, donning masks and changing routines. So many resisted any change, but out of love for those in high risk, others willingly changed their way of life. Such change is what the Gospel always requires, and as we journeyed to the Cross and beyond it, we remembered again that such love always wins.

# From the Mountain to the Valley
Exodus 24:12-18 and Matthew 17:1-9

### Preached on February 23, 2020

LAST WEEK I had the great opportunity to spend some time in Montreat, North Carolina. Montreat was once the headquarters of the Presbyterian Church in the South. It's a special place for a lot of people for several reasons, but it's special for this church because a lot of us went to family camp, a youth conference, or some other conference there. Kelly Dewar, Janice Wolfe, and I were in Montreat last week to attend a small conference on Stewardship, but because it was Montreat, it was also kind of a Presbyterian reunion.

Janice and I were attending the second year of this conference, so we were reuniting with the friends we had made last year. Kelly and I both went to Presbyterian College, so we were catching up with other alums. There were others we knew, and it seemed like even those we didn't know, we at least knew someone whom they knew. I met Bill Sibley of Greenville, South Carolina, who I didn't think I knew but then I learned he was married to our former pastor's daughter.

There were all kinds of connections.

That connectional, reunion type environment is fun to be in because it feels like a family. And that kind of connectional environment is also a little dangerous, because some people remember things I'd rather they forget.

We were sitting at the dinner table with the Rev. Morgan Hay, pastor in Peachtree City, and her husband Robert. Kelly Dewar and I have known both of them since high school. Robert Hay, Jr. now works for the Presbyterian Foundation, a financial institution which serves Presbyterian churches, but more relevant to us, he is a child of this church. His father, Robert Hay, Sr. was the associate pastor for youth here, and if I were to name the top five people who shaped and changed me to become the person I am today, Rev. Robert Hay, Sr. would be in that top five. That's what I was telling the man sitting next to me as a way of explaining how Robert Hay, Jr. and I knew each other. Then Robert said, "And if we were to look back on that time and name the top five kids from that youth group who we thought were least likely to become a Presbyterian minister, I'm not saying that Joe would be at the top of that list, but he would certainly be in it."

Like I said, the environment at Montreat kind of feels like family.

There are people there who remember what I was like growing up and what I was like in college. In some ways I've changed since then, and it's wonderful to remember those people who have helped me change. It's a wonderful thing to have friendships that have lasted through those changes, so I'm thankful that Robert and I, who have known each other since we were teenagers, now can see and respect each other as adults. And the adults we knew then who nurtured us and helped us to grow up can see us now as peers and partners in ministry. That's a big deal. It's a gift, because not everyone who knows your past will ever let you live it down and not everyone loves you enough to help you change and really become who God created you to be.

Our scripture lessons for this morning are all about that kind of change.

This kind of change is infused with profound love.

From the beginning of his life, Moses was being shaped and changed by such love. You know the story. I once saw a bumper sticker that read, "Even Moses started out as a basket case." That's true. He did. Born into a family of enslaved Hebrew people, Moses was placed in a basket by the mother who loved him so much that she made every effort that he be spared from an early death by the hand of his people's oppressors. He floated down the river in that basket and was saved by Pharaoh's daughter. Through a series of other changes, twists and turns, he became a leader of his people. In today's first scripture lesson, he was up on a mountain with God for forty days and forty nights. Maybe you remember that he came down from the mountain changed by this experience, as anyone would be. His skin was glowing because of his proximity to the God of love. Only then he had to interact with his people who had not changed for the better but had reverted back to the kind of idol worship they'd learned back in Egypt and wanted Moses to revert along with them.

Do you have any friends like that?

Friends who love you, only they won't let you change.

Their love drags you down with them.

Thinking of Jesus, there was definitely something about him and his destiny that required him to grow and change, which sometimes made the people who loved him nervous.

His family took a trip to the Temple in Jerusalem, but Jesus went missing because he had left his family to spend time with the learned teachers in their court. He needed to be with those teachers because of his love of God, but his biological family wanted him to come with them. All the time that's how it was. He was coming into his own, changing every day, which sometimes required disappointing or worrying the people who cared about him.

That's life, however.

Love changes us.

Our journeys require change in us.

When we change, sometimes the people who love us have to change along with us.

Today is all about that kind of love.

Today is Transfiguration Sunday. It's the last Sunday of the Church year before Lent begins on Wednesday. It's a Sunday when everything changes for Jesus. He begins to look toward Jerusalem and his death. Before he does, his disciples can see that something has changed. They can tell that God has changed him, and our bulletin cover illustrates it. But what does transfiguration mean?

That prefix, "trans," is a loaded one.

Transfiguration, transformation, transubstantiation - there are all kinds of things that change right before our eyes in miraculous ways. The guidance from Scripture regarding change is this: love changes us, and if it's love that changes, us then go with it.

Let me tell you what I mean.

The second scripture lesson we just read from the Gospel of Matthew tells of how Jesus walked up that mountain seeming to his disciples as fully human. Then at the top he proved himeself fully divine. He was transfigured before them. In the case of Jesus, this was so dramatic a change that it terrified the disciples who saw it. That's understandable because every time someone changes before our eyes we treat it with awe and wonder, but also fear for what that change is going to mean.

It's Peter who I focus on in this Second Scripture Lesson.

I love Peter.

I'm sure you do too.

It's clear that he loves Jesus, but he also is very human. That makes him endearing. You remember how he walked out on the water but started to sink. Later he promised that he would never betray Jesus, but he denied him three times. Peter must have loved Jesus, because once he put it all together: that his friend Jesus really would go from that mountain top down into the valley where he would meet his death, he offered to build three dwellings, one for Jesus, one of Moses, one for Elijah.

Why?

Because Peter wanted to keep Jesus there.

In seeing Jesus standing there with Moses and Elijah, Peter realized that this friend of his was far more than a normal prophet or teacher. In fact, he had been walking around with the very Son of God, who had been one thing, but now would become another. He would not just be preaching sermons and healing the sick. He would also be crushed under the harsh fist of Rome, that he might rise again, conquering sin and death. If that was his destiny, you can understand why Peter wouldn't want him to go through with it. Because Jesus was his friend, you can understand why Peter wanted to keep Jesus in one of those dwellings where he could try and slow down some of the changes that were taking place.

I imagine he was feeling like the mother who watches her son go off to college, knowing that when he comes back, he's going to talk differently. He'll have new ideas in his head, and maybe he'll even be embarrassed of the Appalachian home he was raised in. "Maybe you should just stay here," she says.

Or maybe he was feeling like the girl who hears that a boy wants to ask her twin sister to the dance. She doesn't have a date herself and fears her twin will move on without her. "Maybe we should just stay home and watch a movie instead of going to the dance," she says.

No one wants to lose their son, sister, or friend when change comes to them. That's why we used to write in each other's yearbooks, "Don't ever change." We wrote that because sometimes love means wanting everything to stay the same.

"Can't we just stay here, Jesus? I'll build three dwellings. One for you, one for Moses, and one for Elijah."

That's the feeling parents feel when they want kids to stay where they are and as they are - close by, little, and safe. No one wants their kids getting too big for their britches. Do they? Or better yet, no parent wants their kids getting hurt.

That sounds a lot like love.

I saw a scene on a TV show on Netflix about teenagers that I haven't been able to stop thinking about. One of the teenagers realized that he's not like his friends at school. He's never felt exactly like the other boys he knew. In fact, he's not sure exactly who he is. Still, he wants to go to the school dance, and he wants to wear a head dress like the one his West African mother wears to church, along with eye liner and lip stick. Walking out the door dressed this way his father clearly doesn't want him to go to the dance. Still, his son rushed out. His father rushes toward him and says, "I don't want you to go like this because I love you and I don't want you to get hurt." His son says, "But dad, this is who I am."

The father must decide what to do.

What would love to have him do in this world full of change and transformation, hatred and fear? After a pregnant pause the father finally says, "How is it that my son could be so brave?"

Was Jesus brave? Yes.

Was He loving? Yes.

Was it love for God and his people that caused him to change up on that mountain top and to come down from it ready to face His death? Absolutely.

"Why can't we just stay here Jesus? I'll build three dwelling places, one for you, one for Moses, and one for Elijah?" Peter asked.

"Why can't we stay here?" we all ask.

We ask, because sometimes love demands that we change. However, if it's love that's calling us to be transformed than we must be bold to listen and obey.

I enjoyed so much an article that came from Dr. Nelson Price this morning in the paper. Dr. Price was quoting all the statistical data on demographic changes in our county. We are more diverse than ever, but less religious.

Why?

1.4% of our county is Presbyterian, and I bet most of them only come to church on Christmas and Easter. Why is that and what do we do about it?

Could it be that God is calling us down from the mountain and into the valley that we might make His love for all people plain, but we are still busy building dwelling places?

Could it be that God calls us to be shaped and changed by love, but we resist it?

Could it be that love is transforming us, but we want to stay the same?

If so, we have a friend in Peter. But like him, we must listen to the voice of God. According to Dr. Price, "change is the only constant in life," and according to my father-in-law, it was love which transfigured Jesus, and it is love which must transfigure us. Even if it's in the valley that Jesus will be beaten and nailed to a cross. Still, Christ went, and we must go.

Why? Because "Love is being committed to the growth of another."

That's how a man named Bob, who led our conference in Montreat defined it, and I think he's right. While sometimes love looks like being committed to making sure that nothing ever changes, no one ever gets hurt, and the one we love stays right by our side, that's not always love. Sometimes, that's control.

Today is Transfiguration Sunday.

I've seen transfiguring love.

I saw it in my mother on the day she dropped me off at college. She left all of a sudden saying, "If I stay another moment I'm going to start crying and I don't know when I'll stop, so I'm leaving."

I've seen it in a husband whose heart was breaking as he told his suffering wife it was OK for her to go.

I've seen it in Jesus who went down from the mountain to the valley that you and I might live. Amen.

# Have Mercy on Us, O Lord
## Psalm 51 and Isaiah 58:1-12

**Preached on February 26, 2020 – Ash Wednesday**

TODAY, ANDY Tatnall told me that as he was leaving his office, he overheard two young men talking by the elevator. One asked the other, "What's wrong with your forehead?"

After worshipping this evening there may be some who ask you the same question. "What's wrong with your forehead?"

"Why the ashes?"

"Why the cross?"

Our worship service began with a call to worship where Rev. Cassie Waits said: "Having received the waters of baptism…" Then, we responded: "We come to be marked now with ashes."

Among all the many countercultural rituals within the Christian tradition, this is one of the big ones. While the rest of the world makes up excuses, tonight we can be honest and tell the truth. We are not whole. We are not perfect. We are not innocent or in control.

We do not have it all together, but we do know the one who holds us all in his hands.

We are not good, but we know one who is.

Having claimed us as His in our baptism, we are now bold to stand before God not as we present ourselves to the world, but as we truly are.

"What's wrong with your forehead?" is one question, but tonight we confess that there is something wrong, and not just with our forehead.

Some people hide what's wrong. Not tonight.

Many people have an aversion to the truth.

Others are in the habit of exaggeration or falsehood.

I had a doctor once who asked me when I had stopped taking my prescription. I told him I stopped about a week ago. Then there was silence, which made me nervous. "Actually, it was three weeks ago," I told him because I folded under the pressure. He said, "I already assumed that when you said one week you meant three, because I always multiply by three whatever my patients say because most of them are lying."

Lying to the doctor? What good does that do?

Our doctors are trying to help us. Still we even withhold the truth from them.

The same is true for the dentist.

"Have you been flossing," my dental hygienist asked me.

In the dentist's chair there's really no point in denial. Why? Because if you haven't been flossing your gums will bleed and she can tell that you haven't been flossing like you should.

Still, there's a temptation to withhold the truth and I wonder if we know how much we hurt ourselves when we don't tell the truth to those who are trying to help us.

Of course, it's hard to understand that.

As a kid, I knew what would happen if I confessed the truth to my parents.

When I turned 14 years old, all I wanted for my birthday was a spend the night party. My parents let me invite all my friends. There were a bunch of us, and after watching two or three movies, we decided to sneak into the neighborhood swimming pool. We were able to jump the fence, and after swimming some, one of my friends had the bright idea to throw a pool chair into the water. So, we all tried it. Next thing you know, all the furniture that was around the pool was underwater. Maybe it wasn't such a great idea, but no one saw us do it, so after a little more delinquent behavior, we all went back to my house and fell asleep.

The next morning someone had to pull all those chairs out of the pool.

I feel bad about that… now. At the time all I really cared about was not getting caught. Maybe two days after the incident, someone on the neighborhood association mentioned to my parents how all the pool chairs were found underwater in the pool. "When were they found?" I can imagine my parents asking, while they slowly realized the coincidence that something like that would happen on the same night they hosted a pack of 14-year-old boys in their home. In that moment, sensing that something bad was about to happen, I began to brainstorm an alibi. Then I called my two closest friends so we could get our stories straight should all our parents interrogate us. Little did we know that each of us telling the exact same story smelled like a conspiracy, but we couldn't confess. After all, just imagine what our parents would do to us!

The only outcome of telling the truth that I could foresee was punishment.

I couldn't imagine anything good could come out of getting caught. I wasn't thinking about putting things right again or how guilty I would feel if all the pool furniture rusted from spending the night underwater.

Of course, when our lies fell apart and we got caught, I felt relief.

I didn't realize that I was already being punished by living in a lie.

The truth did set me free, but it's not always that easy.

The truth will set you free so long as the punishment doesn't kill you.

The truth will set you free if the one you are accountable to loves you and wants what's best for you.

Of course, that's not always the case.

Have you ever worked in a place where the culture of denial and blame is so rampant that it matters less what you get done and more that you never mess up? Problems are raised in meetings and no one can reach a solution for everyone responds with either excuses or blame.

In business, a culture of fear is often symptomatic of a vengeful boss.

It's so often true that those to whom we feel accountable are so vengeful that we choose to continue in the lie, the denial, or the suffering.

Such is the case in the medical world, where malpractice insurance is essential.

It feels as though our litigious society wants a payout more than an apology, and a pound of flesh rather than a change of heart.

What's a person to do in such an environment?

You can't just confess, can you?

You can't always wear your heart on your sleeve or broadcast your sinfulness on your forehead.

It might be the case in your family, your job, or your school that it's best to pretend. Certainly, we have created a political environment where denial and blame are more rewarded than honesty and apology. Still, do not be confused, for we Christians are not just accountable to the masses. We are accountable to our God, and who is this God we are accountable to?

Who is this God who claimed us in baptism?

And how will our God react to our repentance and confession?

We read from the Prophet Isaiah:

*Is not this the fast that I choose:*

*To loose the bonds of injustice, to undo the thongs of the yoke, to let the oppressed go free, and to break every yoke?*

The Prophet Isaiah reminds us that our God is not like the nominees for president who will capitalize on our vulnerability, expose our voting record, and be sure that everyone remembers our worst mistakes.

The Prophet reminds us that our God will not use our repentance as a means to gain an upper hand.

God will not use our testimony to take as much from us as He possibly can. No! God hears our confession and rejoices in our fasting because when we finally tell the truth about our brokenness we will begin to heal.

Our God rejoices in confession, for our God wants to give us all that our sins hold us back from.

*If you remove the yoke from among you,*

*The pointing of the finger, the speaking of evil,*

*If you offer your food to the hungry and satisfy the needs of the afflicted, then your light shall rise in the darkness and your gloom will be like the noonday.*

*The Lord will guide you continually, and satisfy your needs in parched places, make your bones strong; and you shall be like a watered garden, like a spring of water, whose waters never fail.*

For our God is ever more ready to forgive than we are to confess, and our God is more interested in the spiritual health of our souls than our dental hygienist is our gums, or my internist is in my cholesterol. All God cares about is giving you and me the mercy that we need should we finally be honest about the brokenness that's killing us.

An old, time-tested sermon illustration goes something like this:

Mrs. Jones dies and stands before the pearly gates. St. Peter looks her up in the Book of Life and sees that Mrs. Jones has several infractions. She was not a good neighbor to Mr. and Mrs. Brown. "Well, they were always rude to me," she tells St. Peter.

"But what about your will. It appears you left everything to your physical therapist Bruno and nothing to the church and nothing to your children?"

"Well, the preacher never came to visit me, and my children get on my nerves. Bruno has been trying to buy himself his own tanning bed and I want to help him out."

"Wait, Mrs. Jones. Look right here. It says that your daughter tried to reconcile with you, but you wouldn't even take her calls because you didn't like the boy who she married. That the preacher tried to call you, but you were too mad at him to pick up because they got new hymnals at the church and you liked the old ones. Now, are those good reasons to ignore these people? It also looks like you owe the girl scouts $32 for six boxes of Samoas, that you never returned a dress your sister let you borrow, and you failed to report a fair amount of cash you received from greyhound racing in your 2019 tax return."

Having run out of excuses, finally, Mrs. Jones kneeled before St. Peter saying, "Have mercy on me, O Lord, for I have sinned." In that moment Saint Peter opened the gate. "Right this way Mrs. Jones. Right this way."

Who is this God of ours?

Is our God like the dental hygienist?

Like our parents, trying to discipline us?

Like our boss, looking for someone to blame?

Like the papers, looking for a good scandal?

Or like a savior, offering us grace, if we would just ask for it?

The flowers on the cover of your bulletin are the work of our own Marilyn Tucker. They illustrate so well our God's intention for what we become:

That we be like a watered garden.

Not a parched earth.

Not an arid landscape.

Not a shame-filled valley or a guilt-ridden pit, but a spring of water whose waters never fail. So, with boldness let us pray:

*Have mercy on me, God, according to your steadfast love;*

*According to your abundant mercy blot out my transgressions.*

# Seeking the Light by Night
## Numbers 21:4-9 and John 3:1-21

### Preached on March 8, 2020

THIS IS the first of four Sundays where the second scripture lesson is from the Gospel of John. As you know, each of the four Gospels tells us the same story, that of the life and ministry of Jesus Christ, in slightly different ways. The Gospel of John offers us a beautiful perspective all its own, with developed characters like Nicodemus, as well as important and subtle details. For example, Nicodemus went to see Jesus at night.

Why would the Gospel of John include this detail?

It's as though we're meant to ask: Why did he go at night? Why was it that didn't go during the day, when people would have seen him, but at night, when people wouldn't have noticed?

This detail is important, and it makes me think how people often things at night do that they would rather not be caught doing during the day. Certainly, what we do in private is not necessarily bad. Think about it. What do you do in private that you're too self-conscious to do in the light of day?

How many sing in the shower, but not in the choir?

How many painters are among us who would have to be forced to put their artwork on the cover of the bulletin, not for lack of talent, but for some other reason? How many of you only paint or sing or dance when no one is looking?

How many students only ask questions of the teacher once the class has left the room?

How many are glad to talk about sports, economics, or movies with whomever, but will only speak of matters of the heart in private with those whom they trust?

Nicodemus went to see Jesus at night. He wouldn't have told his wife where he was going. He waited until he could just slip away.

Why? Why was it at night that he went to see the Lord?

The answer is there in Scripture: "Now there was a Pharisee named Nicodemus, a leader of the Jews." That's just one sentence, but it's plenty of information. I've been wondering why was it that a Pharisee named Nicodemus, who was a leader of the Jews, went to Jesus at night. The more precise question is, if he went at night, what was it that he stood to lose had someone seen him at the doorstep of the Lord?

The answer to that question is obvious when you think about it. A Pharisee, a leader of the Jews, could no more go and see Jesus than an orthopedist could be seen in the office of a chiropractor. How would it look if Lindsey Graham or Lamar Alexander were spotted at a Bernie Sanders rally? It would look about the same as when we were introduced to Segregationist Senator Strom Thurmond's mixed-race daughter Essie Mae Washington.

There are lines drawn to divide society.

What we don't always realize is that those lines often divide our own souls in two.

Nicodemus was a Pharisee, a leader of the Jews, who snuck off to see Jesus. He had to decide which version of himself would go out in the light of day the following morning.

That's how it is for so many of us.

To me, the saddest place in Atlanta is a parking lot that overlooks Piedmont Park. When we were first married, we lived there. We had a small dog in a small apartment on Briarcliff. Sara and I would often take the dog on walks through Piedmont Park and we'd always park in this one parking lot where men sat waiting in their cars. I have an idea what they were waiting for, and I have an idea of the lives that they would leave the parking lot and go back to. They were probably bankers with families and wives. What were they doing in that parking lot, then? Well, they were one person in the light of day and another in the shadow. They were one person when people were looking and another when they snuck off by themselves. Who were they truly? That's one of the great questions of human existence. Another is: what would it take for them to be their shadow selves out in the light of day?

You've seen that kind of coming-out before, often after someone has had a few too many drinks. There's a Latin expression: In vino veritas. Or "In wine lies the truth." Another way to say it is, "I'm one drink away from telling everyone what I really think."

Social scientists tell us that we're not necessarily more honest because of what we've had to drink, we're just less likely to process the consequences of our being honest.

We're not always honest.

No, we're not always honest with ourselves or our neighbors about who we truly are because our standing in the community sometimes matters more to us than even our own happiness. We worry about what people think, always. We worry about what people will say, most of the time. We worry about being exposed, constantly, because we don't want to lose our place in our families, churches, clubs, or neighborhoods. Nicodemus was a Pharisee, a leader of his people, but he was drawn to the light. He just couldn't seek it out when people were looking.

Why? That's easy.

He didn't want to jeopardize his standing in the community.

He didn't want to lose his corner office, his pension fund, or his membership at the Pharisee Country Club with the best golf course that overlooks the Jordan River.

It was at night, then, that he said, "Rabbi, we know that you are a teacher who has come from God; for no one can do these signs that you do apart from the presence of God." Was that good enough? Was that honest enough? By saying this was he stepping out of the shadow enough to benefit from his proximity to the light? Maybe. Maybe not.

Do you remember that movie, *Dead Poets Society*? It's a great teacher movie. The teacher, Robin Williams, is the hero. I like it when the teacher is the hero. I prefer when the preacher is the hero, but I'm glad when the teacher is. What's funny about this movie is that during the day the students at this school wear ties and jackets because they go to a fancy, all boys, private, boarding school where they are being prepared to live as upstanding socialites. A few of them, at night, sneak out of their dorms to read poetry.

You can think of all kinds of things boys at a boarding school might sneak out at night to do, but this group sneaks out to read poetry. That's what they did, and feeling some level of liberation from this experience, one of the members of the Dead Poet's Society takes things farther than the rest of them. He doesn't just read poetry at night while preparing to be like his father during the day. He wants to be who he is at night all the time and tries out for a play knowing that his father, who forbid his passion for acting, might find out. That's a risky thing for a young man to do.

Depending on how you look at it, this young man, in perusing this one thing, either lost everything or gained everything. Nicodemus was the same, but he wasn't a young man. On the cover of your bulletin is this perfect original painting of Nicodemus by our own Jeff Surace. In it, Nicodemus is an old man with a beard. He is as I imagine he was at the time of our second scripture lesson. That's the probable reality of the situation: an old man, experienced, respected, upstanding in the eyes of his people, sneaking out of his house to glimpse the light of the world. What was that costing him? Possibly, he was risking everything.

So, when Jesus answered him, "Very truly, I tell you, no one can see the kingdom of God without being born from above," it must have made perfect sense while being completely confusing. Born. Did he say born? Nicodemus can't again be born, can he? Nicodemus asked him, "How can anyone be born after having grown old? Can one enter a second time into the mother's womb and be born?" Every mother who ever read this has always thought, "Oh gosh, I hope not." But that's not what Jesus means. This isn't like the first time you were born, because it's not the mother who's in pain this time. When it comes to being born again, it's the child who must go through the pain. The child must be ready to step out into the light, leaving behind his honors and titles, security and high standing, to become again like an infant dependent on the grace of his Savior.

Counting the cost, Nicodemus had to ask, "How can these things be?" So, Jesus answered him, "Are you a teacher of Israel, and yet you do not understand these [most basic] things? [Let me teach you something you should know already.] Just as Moses lifted up the serpent in the wilderness, so must the Son of Man be lifted up, that whoever believes in him may have eternal life."

We read about that serpent in the wilderness in our first scripture lesson. Moses had to raise up something that his people might step out from the shadow and be healed. In the same way, Christ was willing to be raised up on a cross himself, that his people would live. That they might live, he called them to step out into the light, finally giving up their relentless pursuit of trying to earn the love of the world, which we will never gain, to accept the love of God, which we don't have to do anything for. "For God so loved the world that he gave his only Son, so that everyone who believes in him may not perish but may have eternal life. Indeed, God did not send the Son into the world to condemn the world, but in order that the world might be saved through him." There it is. Can you accept it?

It's different, because the world is always telling us what we must do to gain love. The world says that to be loved we must have money, power, status, and acceptance. On the other hand, God is always saying, "You already have it. Stop trying so hard. Just step out into the light. Even if you lose all those things you will have gained everything."

The Great Reformer, Martin Luther, called that one verse, John 3:16, the Gospel in miniature, because this is all you really need to know, "God so loved the world that he gave his only son." You've heard it before but listen to this: it's really all about light and darkness.

"And this is the judgement, that the light has come into the world, and people loved darkness rather than light." Why? Appearances. Power. Control. Because sin is not so different from the Coronavirus. It thrives on denial. It grows in the shadow. It spreads when people hide from the light of day and choose to be accepted by their peers, rather than wear a mask or take this disease seriously. So, I charge you today to step out into the light, for He is everything He says He is and more. And love is yours if you'll just accept it.

Grace is yours.

Forgiveness is yours.

Just step out into the light and see that what you stand to lose is nothing compared with what you stand to gain.

Amen.

# Water at Noon
## Exodus and John 4:5-42

### Preached on March 15, 2020

THIS IS the second sermon in a group of four based on these long accounts from the Gospel of John. I just read from verse 5 to verse 42. Rarely would I read 37 verses at one time, but to get the full story we have to read the full story. So, this morning we have another moving and beautiful moment in the ministry of Jesus for our second scripture lesson.

This one is not so unlike the reading from last week, nor is it unlike the reading that will be for next week, in the sense that, consistent with the entire Gospel of John, there is an ongoing theme of darkness and light, a highly developed character in this unnamed woman at the well, and there's an important but subtle detail that the author includes which we shouldn't overlook.

You might remember that last Sunday the detail from the Gospel of John was that Nicodemus, a Pharisee and leader of the Jews, went to visit Jesus at night. I believe the Gospel of John tells us that he went at night because he didn't want to be exposed. Had he been seen at the doorstep of Jesus, he would have risked all kinds of things: rights, privileges, status, or relationships. He couldn't go to visit this radical Savior during the day, because had he been seen with Jesus, he might have lost his place at the top of his religious order. He might even have been rejected by his community.

What we know about this woman at the well, based on one subtle detail, is that she never had these things, or she already lost them.

She was already at the bottom.

She had already been rejected.

She had already fallen down the social ladder because of who she was and what she'd done.

We know that because when Jesus was thirsty, he went to this well at noon, and she was the only one to meet him there. That's the important but subtle detail: noon. The Gospel of John tells us what time it was because the time tells us something about this woman.

That Jesus went to the well when he was thirsty at noon is not surprising. What's surprising is that this woman was there at that time of day. Prompted by the text, we must ask why, and I tell you, it's because in the middle of the day, when the sun was at its highest, was the time when no one else would be there.

That means she's like the woman who quit going to *Weight Watchers* and started just weighing-in in her bathroom because the numbers were going in the wrong direction at the weekly weigh-ins and she didn't want everyone there to see that she was gaining weight instead of losing it.

It means she's like the man who kept being criticized for drinking too much at parties. Because he felt powerless to do anything about it, he started drinking by himself at home.

What happened to this woman?

Why was she at the well at noon?

Well, having tried and failed, she finally gave up.

They whispered behind her back, but she knew what they were saying.

She's the aunt, sister, or daughter who's been married five times and has settled for a sixth because everyone says she's trash and she started to believe them. Without enough pride to resist, but enough to know she doesn't have to be there when they say it, she started going to the well at noon.

Now, this all happened about 2,000 years ago, but still, you probably know her because the same thing still happens all the time. Do you know the woman at the well? I feel sure that you do, because while now we drink water out of bottles instead of out of wells, we still push some people outside the circle, and those of us who are on the inside keep quiet because we know what will happen if we don't.

Nicodemus was that way.

He went to Jesus at night because he didn't want to end up like this woman at the well.

Her story is a classic tragedy that's been relived and retold again and again.

From high school English class, you might remember Hester Prynne with that scarlet letter "A" broadcasting her sin for all to see. Everyone in town knew her story. Everyone knew what she had done. Everyone knew everything about her. Even visitors to her town knew to keep their distance because of the scarlet letter "A" she was forced to where. Unlike Hester Prynne, this woman at the well bore no obvious distinction. Maybe she assumed that Jesus was too thirsty to know he shouldn't be asking her for anything. Maybe she thought he was too desperate to know it would hurt his reputation just to be seen with her. Still, there he was, by her side, at noon. What he said to her is funny: "Give me a drink."

You would think that Jesus would say "Please," but he didn't.

"Give me a drink," he said, which is a funny thing to ask of a person who was widely pitied and never needed.

"Give me a drink," is a funny thing to request from a woman who everyone talked about, but no one wanted to be seen with.

"Give me a drink," is a radical request when you consider that if Moses could strike a rock with a stick and make water come out, then Jesus could have snapped his fingers and Perrier would have fallen from the clouds. Still, to this woman, first of all, he spoke, which was something. Second of all, he asked her for help, which was something else.

I've been thinking and thinking about what Jesus does here, because I understand what's going on with this woman more than I understand what was going on in the mind of the Son of God. I think that's because our society is pushing all of us into this place that the woman at the well found herself in.

Right now, two words well describe our situation: isolation and fear.

It's hard to know what we, as the church, should do in a situation like this one. Having watched the news last Thursday night, Rev. Cassie Waits called so we could talk about it. Together we began discussing what we should do about having church today. We talked about schools closing, even the NBA shutting down. After talking with Cassie, I called some other staff members. I called Rev. Joe Brice, the Sage of Paulding County. After talking about quarantine and lowering the curve he told me that this was a good Sunday to preach the Gospel, because the isolation we're all being pushed into this Sabbath Day isn't so different from the isolation that society is always pushing us towards.

He's right.

We need to gather, but it's always a temptation to stay home. Not just now. It's always a temptation. So also, we need our neighbors, but we're always fearful about reaching out to them, whether they might carry the virus or not.

We crave community, but shame and anxiety are always telling us we'll be rejected.

Then we don't like how things are, but we feel powerless to do anything about it. Even without the voluntary quarantine, the well is the place that our 21st century was already driving us towards because social distancing isn't anything new.

Neither is it anything new for the future to feel so uncertain.

Nor is it a new feeling to feel like we must walk the lonesome valley by ourselves.

Only wait and listen.

Wait just a minute, for along comes Jesus saying, "Give me a drink."

For her, after that request, a theological discussion ensued. What their discussion came down to was that Jesus told the woman he knew who she was. He wasn't talking with her because he was naïve. He knew where she had been, what she'd done, and how many men she'd been married to. He told her that he knew how she worshiped at the wrong place and was looking for salvation in the wrong places. She couldn't hide anything from the people of her community because they already knew, and this new guy knew it all and went to her any way.

It wasn't because he was ignorant that he spoke to her. It was because he was different.

Then she said to him, "I know that Messiah is coming. When he comes he will proclaim all things to us." Having already done that he said, "I am he, the one who is speaking to you." After that the woman left her water jar and went back to the city, and listen to what she said, "Come and see a man who told me everything I have ever done! He cannot be the Messiah, can he?" You know what changed with that announcement?

The woman who had been all alone ran towards the city. The one who had nothing to offer brought her people the greatest news that's ever been heard, and the Lord who came to the well thirsty, asking for water, never even got a sip.

I feel sure that was just fine with Jesus, because he's never so concerned with his own wellbeing so much as he's concerned with the wellbeing of our whole world. Jesus was thirsty, but he's calling on us to offer to the world a sip of water. And like her, we must be convinced that we have any right to do it.

Because she convinced her of her innate worth, she became someone different. She was no longer confined by what the world said about her but was transformed by the power of Christ. Because of the Good News, she became not the one who everyone talked about, but one who changed her entire village by what she had to say.

She wasn't alone.

Christ was with her.

And she wasn't powerless, but powerful.

The change that happened within this woman at the well reminds me of the words of Marianne Williamson:

*Our deepest fear is not that we are inadequate.*

*Our deepest fear is that we are powerful beyond measure.*

*It is our light, not our darkness that most frightens us.*

*We ask ourselves,*

*Who am I to be brilliant, gorgeous, talented, fabulous?*

*Actually, who are you not to be?*

*You are a child of God.*

*Your playing small does not serve the world.*

*There is nothing enlightened about shrinking so that other people won't feel insecure around you. We are all meant to shine, as children do.*

*We were born to make manifest the glory of God that is within us.*

*It's not just in some of us; it's in everyone.*

*And as we let our own light shine, we unconsciously give other people permission to do the same.*

*As we are liberated from our own fear, our presence automatically liberates others.*

I heard that quote in a movie Lily and I were watching yesterday morning. Hearing it, I was reminded that Jesus is all the time interrupting our solitude, hopelessness, and fear to remind us that our most basic words and most simple efforts bring to the world faith, hope, and love.

In these strange times, will you tell his story?

Will you live his truth?

Amen.

# Surely, We Are Not Blind, Are We?
## Psalm 23 and John 9:1-41

**Preached on 3/22/20**

Do you remember when we used to go out to dinner?

I do, and I'm trying to remember the bad things about going out to dinner so I don't miss it so much.

Have you ever been out to dinner with another couple and he or she won't let him or her finish telling a story for correcting some insignificant detail?

Do you know what I'm talking about?

It annoys me, because it seems petty, and it always really bothers me when the details prevent the telling of a good story. For example, maybe she was trying to tell you how she was walking the dog across the street and Fido was out in front and in the middle of the crosswalk when a blue Ford Mustang turned the corner too quickly and… "No, it was a red Dodge Charger," he interrupts her to say.

In this instance, the thing that drives me crazy is I don't care what color the car was. I care whether or not the dog got run over. Do you know what I mean?

It's not uncommon for people to get caught up in details.

Details are important.

Many good story tellers say, "I never let the truth get in the way of a good story." That might be too extreme. I do know that details are important. We can't ignore them. However, sometimes we allow little details to distract us from big truths.

Our second scripture lesson began: "As he walked along, he saw a man blind from birth. His disciples asked him, 'Rabbi, who sinned, this man or his parents that he was born blind?'"

Jesus answers, "Who cares?"

That's not exactly what he said, but it's close enough.

What I believe he was trying to say is, "Don't be distracted by the details. Watch what I'm about to do." Then, Jesus "spat on the ground and made mud with the saliva and spread the mud on the man's eyes, saying to him, 'Go, wash in the pool of Siloam'. Then he went and washed and came back able to see."

That's what's pictured on the cover of your bulletin.

Again, a member of our own community, Bill Needs, took the time to contribute his gifts that we might stand back in awe and wonder at Jesus, beholding this great miracle. He titled his work, "One thing I do know, I was blind and now I see."

That's the main thing.

He got it.

What about everyone else?

After the man went and washed and came back able to see, "the neighbors and those who had seen him before as a beggar began to ask, 'Is this not the man who used to sit and beg?'"

Some were saying, "It is he."

Others were saying, "No, but it is someone like him."

He kept saying, "I am the man."

But they kept asking him.

Why were they asking, and why weren't they rejoicing? Well, they were caught up in the details, unable to see the miracle that had just taken place.

Before that the disciples, so focused on the problem, and so practiced in assigning blame and debating "who sinned" to cause the man's blindness, were about to gloss right over the miracle. Then the Pharisees get involved, and when Pharisees get involved there's always trouble. They got stuck on the fact that it was a Sabbath day when Jesus made the mud and opened his eyes, and so they boldly proclaim: "This is not from God, for he does not observe the Sabbath."

Now, why did that matter?

Why an interrogation and not a party?

Couldn't they just be happy for this man?

Where was the cake and the parade celebrating the day when the man born blind regained his sight?

Instead, the investigation continues.

Why? Because a culture trained to look for sin can be blind to miracles.

A culture focused on details can ignore the bigger picture.

A culture concerned with who did it or who is trying to do it can become distracted from what happened or what needs to happen.

That's how it happened then, and that's how it is now.

Have you been listening to all the criticism?

Have you heard what should have happened and who should have done what and when?

Have you heard that this whole Corona thing is just the Democrat's attempt to get President Trump out of office? Have you heard that sales of Corona beer have slumped? Rather than just listen to the CDC or the governor, we get caught up in debates. We trip over details.

Then we get into the blame part: Why do all these things start in China? Shouldn't the President have done something before now? Why are people still going to the beach?

It's because they drank water out of the hose as a kid and heard that makes you immune to it. You know, the priority here should be caring for people rather than assigning blame.

The goal should be eliminating disease rather than talking about what our leaders could have done better.

Maybe that's where we'll get eventually, but to get there, we have to stop acting like unpleasant dinner guests, or worse, Pharisees.

I hate Pharisees.

Don't you?

Unfortunately, I am one.

Like them, I get more interested in whose fault it was.

I wander down these rabbit holes that distract me from the real issue. I become problem-focused, rather than solution-focused, sin-focused rather than miracle-focused, detail-focused rather than big-picture focused, and when that happens I can't be surprised if nothing ever gets done and if life feels more like a deposition rather than the celebration God created it to be.

Look again at our second scripture lesson. First, the Disciples want to know who sinned. Then the Pharisees want to know when he healed the man. The parents just don't want to offend anybody. Meanwhile, Jesus gave this man sight.

The Pharisees asked, "We are not blind, are we?"

You better believe we are.

But not all of us.

This coronavirus is a source of stress and conflict. Husbands and wives are arguing. Siblings are fighting. Stocks are declining. Employers are having to lay off staff. Last week, my neighbor told me about her friend's aunt who had to ask her maid not to come back, and because Aunt Sally doesn't drive, she also counted on this maid to deliver her vodka, so remember Aunt Sally in your prayers this week. She's having a really hard time.

The truth is that we all have it hard right now, though some of us have it harder than others.

The most challenging phone call I've had to make since this thing started was to Andrew MacIntosh, who's wedding was supposed to be in our sanctuary yesterday. Friday before last, I called him. "Andrew," I said, "We have a problem."

Well, it turned out his caterers were backing out anyway and his guests were already nervous, but if a tear was shed or a harsh word was spoken, I don't know about it. All I know is that Anna, Andrew's bride, asked me if I could still officiate a private service, saying, "We're just excited to be married. The particulars are whatever they need to be."

This has been a hard season for so many reasons. Some of you have had to lay off employees. Others have feared for the future as the stock market dropped. We all have had to change our daily routines. Parents have become teachers, siblings have become playmates because there's no one else to play with, doctors and nurses are working overtime, and we all have felt the lingering anxiety of not knowing.

Every day, I've woken up to a tightness in my chest. Have you?

But let me tell you what I'm forcing myself to see: If our kids are healthy, it's a miracle.

If we have a home to be confined in, we need to give thanks to God.

This service is coming to you in your home because we can't be together, and thanks to the providence of God working through a team of volunteers, this service is streaming to you. We can't be blind to what's good, no matter how frustrating the distractions and the changes. Consider, what are those distractions and changes really? Most of them are just details, and we can't allow the details to distract us from the miracle. If Anna and Andrew can see it as their wedding plans collapse, what's our excuse?

"Surely, we are not blind, are we?"

That's what the Pharisees asked, and they were blind. But we don't have to be.

Open your eyes to miracles.

Open your eyes to God at work among us now.

Amen.

# Dry Bones
Ezekiel 37:1-14 and John 11:1-45

### Preached on March 29, 2020

EVERY NIGHT before we eat supper, we always say one thing that we're thankful for. Everyone has to say something. No one can eat a bite until we've all said at least one thing we are thankful for, no repeats and no kiss-ups. By "kiss-ups" I mean that no one is allowed to say, "I'm thankful for Mama." This is not a time for kissing up, this is a time for gratitude, but while repeats and kissing up are against the rules, simple is OK.

Gratitude doesn't have to be for anything complicated. So, often, we say things like: "I'm thankful we're having macaroni and cheese," or "I'm thankful for my friends." Thinking about it one night last week, I realized that I was thankful for technology, and that's what I said. "I'm thankful for technology."

Now, I'm not usually.

Sometimes I hate it.

I generally prefer things that I can fix without the help of an expert. Or better, I prefer things that I can understand. So now, while I have often hated having a phone that's smarter than me or a car that talks, I'm thankful for technology because it keeps me from feeling separated from all of you.

Today, technology is a tool we can use to fight isolation.

Technology defies social distancing.

Technology can help us beat back fear with love.

It daily reminds us that we're not alone. Which is true, we're not alone, though it's easy now to feel that way, just as it's always been easy to feel that way.

Before this quarantine ever happened, I once felt all alone in one of the biggest, most densely populated cities in the world. I was in New York City, and there I had the chance to volunteer in a great big building where counterfeit clothing was processed and cleaned, then distributed to homeless people. I introduced myself to the man who was supervising the project and told him my name and that I was from Georgia, and he said, "Yeah, I can tell."

In New York City, way up north, I felt like a pilgrim in a barren land of people who used too much diction and not enough y'alls.

I didn't like it. But I never do, because felling alone is the worst.

Worse still was when I spent a summer in Argentina as a missionary intern. I felt alone often there, not because there weren't people around, but because I couldn't always understand what people were saying. I remember riding a train in Buenos Aires, the capital, and up came a Mormon missionary who spoke English. I was so happy to talk with him in a language I could understand that I nearly converted.

"Please, tell me more," I said to this man.

It was probably the first time the missionary was the one trying to get away.

Feeling alone isn't a good feeling. That's why, in this dangerous time where social distancing and fear are combining to assail our spirits, I give thanks for everything that keeps us connected - technology, language, and empathy.

Empathy forges connections today, because we are all feeling the same things. We've had some extra time to clean up around the house, and something that we've kept but keep thinking about getting rid of is a huge collection of *National Geographic* magazines. It's like we have all of them, but it's hard for me to let these magazines go because the pictures on the cover are just so powerful. On these covers, we look into the eyes of the desperate mother, the hungry child, the refugee with the soulful eyes, the smiling groom on his wedding day, and regardless of the culture or ethnicity of the person or the age of the photograph you can tell what each person is feeling by the emotions there on their face. Regardless of the year the picture was taken you can feel a connection.

The same thing is happening right now on Facebook, because people aren't just spouting out what they think on there, as usual. Now they're also posting what they're feeling.

A member of our church recently posted: "How long is this social distancing supposed to last? My wife keeps trying to come in the house."

Do you know the feeling?

Are the people you're quarantined with driving you crazy?

Elsewhere on Facebook, there are the desperate prayers of a mother-turned-teacher, as well as reports from the first day of homeschooling, like: "Both students suspended. Teacher caught drinking on the job."

There are many others.

Religious ones, even.

I saw that someone posted, "I didn't expect to give up quite this much up for Lent."

Seeing and reading this kind of stuff, I know what everyone out there is feeling. It's the same thing I'm feeling. We're in a moment of mass solidarity, because so many of us, regardless of party, race, creed, nationality, or rank on the totem pole, are in this together.

We are not in this thing alone. We have to remember that, because knowing that we're together makes a difference.

That's why the most important lesson for us to hear from today's Gospel reading is in just two words: Jesus wept. These are two words in the older translations. It's "Jesus began to weep" in our pew Bibles, which isn't as succinct. Regardless, it's still among the shortest verses in the Bible, and out of the 45 verses that I just read, that's the one I focus on.

In our second scripture lesson for this morning, Jesus saw Mary's tears. When he saw her crying, he started crying. Why? Because not only are we all in this together, God's in it with us too.

When we see the tears of Christ, we come to know that our God wipes our tears away not with indifference, but with compassion.

When we reveal to our Creator the depths of our hearts and our deepest pain, we know that God is feeling that same pain with us.

Mary looked to him with tears in her eyes to see that he felt the same grief.

Jesus wept.

He was not indifferent.

He hurt. He grieved. He just isn't stuck in it.

Do you know what I mean by that?

Well, to Mary and Martha, all they could see in the world at the beginning of this scripture lesson, all any of us would have been able to see was a dying brother and a miracle-worker who was running late. Then, when they closed him up in the tomb, they were confined to their own understanding of what was possible and what wasn't possible.

What was possible? Healing.

What wasn't possible? Bringing someone back from the dead.

This is how we all think.

The Prophet Ezekiel wasn't any different in our first Scripture Lesson. He saw a valley of dry bones and God asked him, "Mortal, can these bones live?" Ezekiel was far more faithful than I would have been because he said, "O Lord God, you know." That's right. God does know, but sometimes I think I do.

"Will this quarantine ever end?" I ask.

It sure doesn't feel like it.

What started with two weeks is now stretching out to maybe the kids being back to school in May. I doubt it. So, does everyone else. If it felt to anyone else like this was going to end any time soon, half the nation wouldn't have filled up their attics with toilet paper.

We're settling into this crisis, and it's hard to see over the top of it.

You can tell that's the truth because the people who talk about getting past it sound like jerks. Did you hear about the lieutenant governor who wants to just let the grandparents die out so we can get back to normal? If that guy gets reelected, our democracy is in worse shape than our economy. Still, life will go on. We will get past this. And no one need be sacrificed at the Idol of the Dow to do it. Do you know how I know? Because I've just heard about the God who breathed on a pile of dry bones and brought them back to life and Jesus Christ who called into a tomb and a dead man walked out.

Carol Bockman painted it for us on our bulletin cover. Look and see, death is not even the end with our God, so coronavirus will not be, either. You know that. I know that. But we have to act like we know it and come out of this thing better than before, rather than emerge from our caves as pajama-wearing, apathetic, selfish, couch potatoes.

This is a defining moment.

It's a moment, where we have to let go of so much, but don't forget that we will also choose what we'll pick back up once it's over.

What I suggest you pick up now and cling to once it's over is your power.

It was a valley of dry bones and God called on the Prophet Ezekiel to prophesy to them. That was a bold request, to use his words to do something so momentous, but God uses our words all the time to do impossible things. For example, I was running yesterday, and I saw a banner. It said, "Marietta, we can do hard things." I saw another that said, "This too shall pass." Then I saw rainbows in windows because people are trying to give children something to look for as they walk around their neighborhoods.

People are still connecting.

Lives are still changing, and we as a church will come out of this stronger than ever before if we remember that our words can break the silence and do impossible things.

You might be hesitant. Ezekiel was, but don't underestimate what happens when you take the time to speak.

Years ago, my father had a quadrupole bypass surgery. He was in the hospital, and as he had become a critic of the pastor who was serving our church then, he wasn't interested in letting anyone here on the church staff know where he was or what was going on. The pastor came to visit any way, and after the visit my father said, "Joe, it just means something. It just means something when someone takes the time to say they care."

Use your words, First Presbyterian Church.

Use your words, use technology, be honest with each other about your true feelings, just as those who can't get to the salon are having to be honest about their true hair color. And watch as dry bones come to life, as broken relationships are mended once more by the power of the Holy Spirit working among us, connecting us, changing us for the better.

Amen.

# Who is This?
## Psalm 118:1-2 and 19-29, Matthew 21:1-11

### Preached on April 5, 2020 – Palm Sunday

THE GOSPEL lesson for today, and the general spirit of this today, Palm Sunday, reminds me of so many movies or books where something happens: a magic lamp is rubbed, a map is discovered, or a spaceship is boarded and it lifts the characters from their normal lives into adventure, hardship, and eventually triumph.

For Jesus it was a donkey and not a spaceship.

He gets on the donkey and first there's adventure and a cheering crowd, then hardship, eventually triumph, but it all starts with this donkey. According to the Gospel of Matthew it was both a donkey and a colt. Once he's on them, everything changes. That's what's on your bulletin cover – a painting of Jesus's view as he begins his journey into the city of Jerusalem.

He's standing on the cliff.

His next step sets him on a course where everything will change, for him and for the world. Now, because we have heard the story before, we all know what awaits him, and considering his fate, knowing he rides toward the Cross, there's a part of me that wishes he could turn around.

When I was a kid, I had that same feeling watching this cartoon movie called *An American Tail*. The word "tail," in the title is a homophone. Someone listening to this sermon just said, "I can't believe he knows such a big word," but I do, and I had to do something to redeem myself for using a children's cartoon as a sermon illustration. So, I'm using this big word: homophone. In the title it's spelled "t-a-i-l," because this movie is about a little mouse who immigrates from Eastern Europe to America in the hopes of escaping the oppressive cats of his homeland. He goes with his family, but on the way across the sea he chases his hat out on the deck during a storm and he's swept off the boat. He slips through his desperate father mouse's fingers and ends up lost at sea.

I remember watching this movie as a kid over and over, and each time I watched it I wondered he had to chase that stupid hat. But that's because I knew. Had he known where chasing his hat out onto the ship's deck would lead him, maybe he wouldn't have gone after it in the first place.

Movies have to have adventure, so against my advice, the mouse chased the hat and fell overboard. And every Palm Sunday, Jesus keeps riding his donkey into Jerusalem, even though it is in this city that he will meet his death. What's different between the mouse in *An American Tail* and Jesus is that, while the mouse couldn't have known that chasing his hat out onto the deck would lead to him being swept overboard, atop his donkey, Jesus knows.

Jesus knows what's going to happen to him as he rides into Jerusalem, and he goes anyway.

He hears the cheers and sees the waving palms, knowing that they'll soon be shouting, "Crucify him" and yet he goes anyway.

He waves to the crowd, knowing that a nail will pierce both his hands, and still he rides on.

He felt the gentle breeze on his skin knowing that soon his back would be whipped, his head would be crowned with thorns, and still, onward he goes.

He knew, you see, and had it been any of us, we would have turned around.

That's how we are. If we only would have known how challenging the journey, we would have turned around. If only we had stopped travel out of China earlier. If only we had started the quarantine sooner. If only we had listened to the experts. If only we heeded the warnings. I wish we had. I wish we had done all those things, but now it's too late, and as we journey into the unknown, moving forward into the future which we cannot avoid, we only face one choice: Will we face the future with fear, or with faith?

In other words, will we accept our new reality, or live in denial?

Will we adapt, or hide?

Will we search for someone to blame, or will we develop solutions?

Will we blame God, or will we see God at work?

Many in Jerusalem were fearful. "Let's just send him back home. Let's put the genie back in the bottle. Forget about the adventure," they said, though there was no going back. So, when he entered Jerusalem, the whole city was in turmoil, asking, "Who is this?"

That's what everyone asks when the unplanned happens.

That's what everyone wants to know when their world turns upside down.

Who is this that causes such turmoil when all we want is peace and normalcy?

Who is this that gets the crowds so up in arms?

Who is this that topples the tables of money changers, gives the blind their sight, raises dead men from the grave, and tells us that a new Kingdom is coming if we only have the eyes to see it? You know who he is already. He is the King of Kings and Lord of Lords, and what he demands of us today is that we see him at work in the midst of one of the great moments of chaos that we've seen in a generation.

He is the embodiment of Grace, and in the midst of this virus he invites us to recognize that when we are shaped and changed, purified and refined, challenged and broken down it is an invitation to be stronger than we were before. Consider him and remember that it is through adventures that heroes are born.

Maybe you remember that the Wizard Gandalf said to Frodo: "All we have to decide is what to do with the time that is given us," or how Mikey yelled to the Goonies from the tunnel under their hometown: "This is our time." Sure, I wish we had not been given this time. I wish you high school seniors were not missing your graduation and prom. I wish that you parents were not facing lay-offs and uncertainty. I wish that we all were not at risk, but my friends, the hero and the villain swim through the same water. Only one can emerge. Only one will rule this day, and I charge you to follow the one whom death cannot conquer like you've never followed him before.

One way or the other God is going to lead us out of this, and if we walk beside God, God will shape and change us.

We will be made better for this, if we chose to see with the eyes of faith rather than fear.

We will be closer as families. We will be stronger as a church. We will be more faithful Christians, as truly we are tested. You see, the school tests have been canceled to make room for a real one that our children might learn, that they don't have to go through life being afraid that something bad is going to happen, because all things are work together for good.

Know it now, that we are enough, and we have enough because God is enough.

"Who is this?" Jerusalem asked, urging him to turn around lest everything change. My friends, we know who Jesus is, and he knows who we are. So, let us follow him and be changed forever. Amen.

# As Often as You Drink It
## Exodus 12:1-14 and 1 Corinthians 11:23-26

### Preached on April 9, 2020 – Maundy Thursday

THERE'S SOMETHING amazing about the power of a routine.

Do you remember having one?

Saturday used to be the only day when we'd wake up without a fixed agenda. Maybe we'd have pancakes, or maybe not. It didn't matter, because no one had to rush out the door to school. On Saturdays we let our girls watch TV in their PJs, then they ate when they wanted. We'd get irritated during basketball season because it messed all that up. We had to have a schedule on those Saturdays, and we hated it. Now I'd love something to go to on a Saturday because every day is Saturday.

Here it is Spring Break, and what do I miss? I miss our girls' teachers sending them daily assignments to work on.

I miss busy-ness.

I miss rushing out the door.

What do we have to get to?

Somebody told me that after dinner is the time he changes out of his morning PJs to get into his sleeping PJs. Another coined a new word: yogajam. That's the moment of the day when we change out of our yoga pants and into our pajama pants. In this strange season of quarantine and social distancing, the first thing to go in many of our homes was our wardrobe. The second, our rules for watching TV.

Before, so many parents in our church had a limit on the amount of time their children could spend in from of a screen, television or otherwise. Now, we'll let them watch as much as they want if they'll let us get a little work done.

Some things, I'm thankful are gone.

Today, there are no lunch boxes to pack. There are also no spelling tests to study for. There are no practices to drive to and from, no arguments regarding what's appropriate and what's not appropriate to wear to church. But mostly, I miss it all.

For me, what I'm realizing now more than ever, is that a routine gives my life stability.

I like having places to go.

Even though I don't go to the church every day, I still get dressed like I do. Even though I could wear PJs under this robe while I preach, I choose not to, because I'm clinging to every little habit and ritual that might make this strange season seem normal.

Some, today, are dubbed essential. Not all of us, but some of us.

The ones who are considered essential still go to work. They get dressed and face the day. What about the rest of us? What does it mean to be labeled non-essential? What does it mean for those who have the chance to stay home and out of Corona's reach? Surely, staying safe and at home is a blessing and a privilege, but don't we also lose sight of some bit of our core identity when we lose the typical rhythms of wake up early, drink your first cup of coffee, and rush out the door?

Some have said that this is what it's like to retire, and then regret it. Today, we have so much free time that we don't know what to do with it all. After two weeks we'd give anything for something productive to do. Two months of vacation sounds attractive, but how do you know who you are if you don't know what to do?

Here at the church it may feel the same.

We don't gather in person, but on a screen. This is Holy Week, and our choir is home, our congregation is home. There are only a few of us here. Understandably, things are different.

Like some of the rhythms of our home life, some traditions at our church are falling away, others, people are fighting for. Why? I believe it's because many of the rituals of our church are no different than our other routines, jobs, and activities: they all tell us something about who we are.

So, tonight we've fought to maintain something.

Here is a table. It's one that's unlike any other.

Jesus called his disciples to gather around it saying, "Take and eat, this is my body broken for you. Drink this cup, and every time you drink of it, do this in remembrance of me."

What does it mean? Why do we care about it so much that we'd ask you to come to this worship service having set your own table at home with bread from your own pantry and the fruit of the vine from your own bottle?

It's because the Jews kept celebrating Passover, despite famines, wars, and genocides, for it reminded them who they are and who God is.

Can you imagine what it must have been like, in a concentration camp, to remember how God freed our ancestors from oppression?

Can you imagine what it must have been like to sit at table with Ann Frank in the attic and to hear that God has delivered us once before?

Here in Exodus, Chapter 12 the Lord tells Moses and Aaron how and when.

Every year, the feast of Passover "Shall be a day of remembrance for you. You shall celebrate it as a festival of the Lord throughout your generations you shall observe it as a perpetual ordinance."

Every household in the assembled congregation of Israel shall take part, every household shall have a lamb of their own, unless they are too small and need to share with their neighbors.

"This month shall mark for you the beginning of months," says the Lord, "It shall be the first month of the year for you," so that you begin every year by remembering the story that defines who you are. And now we gather with bread and cup in our homes, joined in Spirit, linked by the internet, to remember again that when everything changes, Christ is the same. We do so because Christ is the same. Even when everything changes for you, in God's sight, you are the same.

At this table there is no essential and nonessential, for all are one in Christ Jesus. All are part of the same body. All are one and all are sacred, you and me and every one of us. For regardless of the time or the season, Christ has died for us.

Doesn't that matter more than whether or not we have school or a job to go to?

Doesn't that matter more than whether or not we have a report card coming home?

We have fought for this table tonight. Some of you may be uncomfortable with the idea of serving yourself a sacred meal. It took me a while to get my mind around it and to eventually come to peace with the truth: We fight to keep this table when we aren't allowed to gather around any others because it calls us to judge ourselves by a standard of grace and not of worth. It calls us to recognize that while the world will say that those with the most to do matter the most, Christ says, "I invite you to this table. I died for you, and that matters more than anything else."

In a time of changing rhythms, cancelations, and social distance, remember this table. Take and eat this bread and know who you are. Know what you're worth. Know the truth.

Amen.

# Caiaphas' had a plan
John 18:1-14

## Preached on April 10, 2020 – Good Friday

TO ME, the haunting words of this Good Friday scripture lesson are those of verse 14:

*Caiaphas was the one who had advised the Jews that it was better to have one person die for the people.*

On the surface, that seems like a good plan. It seems better that one man die rather than many, should Rome strike to put down a full rebellion. In the mind of the Empire, the people who assembled in mass on Palm Sunday must be reminded who is in charge. Just do the math. If one can die in the place of many, it would be for the best. Now, maybe it's cold-blooded and calculating to choose one scapegoat, but it's also pragmatic. It's a political choice in the midst of a crisis, and should the ends justify the means, then Caiaphas emerges from the crisis a hero. That's a strange thing to think about, yet we know that Caiaphas is not the hero in this story. Christ is. So, on this Good Friday nearly 2,000 years later, I call on you to recognize with me how the same forces of good and evil are at work in world today - how his plan seems eerily relevant now, as our nation faces a pandemic and the potential for a crashing economy.

Who have you heard talk about sacrificing a few for the good of the whole?

Who have you heard ask that since this virus only effects those who are at risk already, "Why should I let it inconvenience me?"

Then there are the words of Texas Lieutenant Governor Dan Patrick still ringing in my ears, reminding me of how many people in our world today are like Caiaphas even now, willing to allow a few people to die in order to keep commerce operating normally, the economy going, and maintain control. To try and keep the world from changing, in the midst of a viral pandemic, there are those who would allow one person to die for the people.

Of course, this suggestion from Caiaphas was for the greater good.

His words hardly sound sinister on the surface.

Likewise, what the Lieutenant Governor suggested could be interpreted as benevolent. He was saying that grandparents, like him, would be glad to risk their lives for the greater good and the health of the economy. His exact words on Fox News were:

*No one reached out to me and said, 'As a senior citizen, are you willing to take a chance on your survival in exchange for keeping the America that all America loves for your children and grandchildren? If that's the exchange, I'm all in.'*

This statement of his is pragmatic.

In a sense, it's selfless and even loving, but it's also idolatrous. In creating this plan, he places the fate of this nation in his own hands and abandons the principles which our nation and our faith rests on. He need not have come up with such a plan, for when the children sing, "He's got the whole world in his hands," they're not singing about the Lieutenant Governor. The fate of our nation rests not in the hands of any mortal, but in the hands of Christ who reigns.

What the world needs to hear now is that grandparents don't need to die for the good of this country. In fact, if they sacrifice themselves for the good of the American economy, then we have become a nation with a far greater problem than the one we face right now. What good has been accomplished if we emerge from this crisis having forfeited our souls?

On this Good Friday, we come face to face with the reality that the same corruption which put Christ on the cross still infects us.

While the sidewalks are empty, sin still walks the streets of our city and the halls of our Congress.

We are not immune to idolatry, nor the virus. On this Good Friday we must face the reality that when a problem creeps up, we must call on God to guide us, lest our treatment cause even greater harm.

For when we sacrifice one for the good of many, are we truly loving our neighbor as ourselves?

When we consider putting our loved ones at risk for the good of our economy, who is our God?

If we work to prop up a broken system, work tirelessly to keep everything just as it always has been, or connive to pragmatically appease Rome or any other power just to get things back to normal, how will anything ever change for the better?

*Tied to What is Below*

I served a church in Columbia, Tennessee before returning here, to this church where I grew up. Columbia, Tennessee is home to many incredible people, many strong Christians and many outstanding churches. It's from Columbia that I got this idea to ask neighboring churches to gather together during Holy Week as we have this week, each pastor taking a different day to lead the service that a Christian community be formed as we journey to the cross together. Columbia is a wonderful place, but there was one story not many people liked to tell - that of the Race Riot of 1946.

It started when a young Black man pushed a white store clerk through a window. The clerk was rude to his mother, and the young man couldn't take it.

Once word spread a length of rope was purchased.

A white mob assembled at the courthouse.

It would have been easy for the Black community in Columbia to turn the young man over the mob, thinking that it is better to have one person die for the people, but that's not what they decided to do.

Having had enough of lynching, knowing that evil is a bottomless pit which will never be satisfied and that allowing this one to die would only lead to more, the Black community mobilized, hid the young man, set up posts of armed men on the roofs of buildings, and readied themselves to fight the white mob to save this one young man. Interestingly, not a shot was fired. Not a single person, white or black was killed. So many Black men were locked up in the jail that Thurgood Marshall came to town. He worked for justice in that Tennessee town, and when it was over, he so feared for his life that a driver snuck him out of Columbia in the trunk of a car.

The church I served in Columbia held a community worship service marking the 70th anniversary of these events. Near the close of the service a young man stood up and asked to speak. He told us how he was able to meet Thurgood Marshall before his death, after he had been appointed to the Supreme Court. The young man said, "Justice Marshall, I just want to thank you for what you did for my hometown in Columbia, Tennessee. Things are a lot better now. They're not perfect, but they're better. You did a lot of good." The Justice asked, "To get up here to Washington D.C. from Columbia, did you have to sneak out in the trunk of a car?"

"No, sir," he said.

"Then I guess I did do some good," the Supreme Court justice responded.

My friends, if we want to see our world change for the better, we have to abandon those plans which require us to preserve our lives at the cost of our souls.

We must honor the sacredness of every human life, for not one is disposable.

We cannot put ourselves in the place of God, abandoning the principles which he taught us.

For rather than keep people quiet so that Rome would be satisfied, Christ wants us shouting "halleluiahs" and ushering in the Kingdom of God.

Rather than maintain what is for the good for the grandchildren, Christ wants a new heaven and a new earth with no oppression and no more Rome.

What Caiaphas didn't understand is that Rome will never be satisfied. So, when we sacrifice people to earthly powers, either the empire or the economy, we are bowing before idols who cannot sustain us and will only grow hungry for human flesh again. We can no more manipulate the Dow than Caiaphas and his council could assuage the Roman empire, for they were fickle and heartless. Meet their demands today and just be prepared for the cost to rise tomorrow. If we are willing to give up our grandparents for the good of the economy, then we may stand to save our stocks while losing our souls.

The alternative my friends is this: hope.

Not pragmatism.

Not bargaining.

Not compromise.

Not an early death for some for the greater good, but eternal life for all.

In the midst of this strange time, the promise is the same though it rings true in a new way. It's not just survival that he offers, but as the hymn says:

*It's strength for today and bright hope for tomorrow.*

*It's pardon for sin and a peace that endureth.*

*It's His own dear presence to cheer and to guide.*

*It's blessings, all ours, and ten thousand beside.*

Why? Because his faithfulness is great, and his mercies are boundless.

He faces death not to appease Rome or for the good of the Dow, but to show the powers of the earth that they are powerless and to prove to you and to me that we need not bow before a culture of materialism and oppression. The life that he offers is the only one worth having. Today we remember that this one died for all people, and not one more needs to die for us to be saved.

Alleluia.

Amen.

# He is Risen!
## Psalm 114 and Matthew 28:1-10

### Preached on April 12, 2020

TODAY IS the most important day of the Christian calendar because today we celebrate Christ's victory over death. However, today also brings with it one of the most challenging claims Christianity makes. Namely, that Jesus Christ rose from the dead.

Not everybody believes that.

Thomas Jefferson didn't.

He was what some would call a cafeteria Christian. Like going through the line at Piccadilly, picking and choosing, he took his Bible and his scissors and he left in the teachings of Christ he most admired, literally cut out the parts of the story he couldn't believe, and made for himself what today is known as The Jefferson Bible. Of course, this version leaves out the resurrection. Not everyone believes in a bodily resurrection. Not everyone believes in it today, not everyone did back in 1776, and even on Easter morning 2,000 years ago, not everyone believed that Jesus would rise from the dead. Certainly, the disciples didn't.

You can tell from how our second scripture lesson began, that the disciples did not believe he would rise from the dead on that Easter morning nearly 2,000 years ago. We know that they didn't because they're nowhere near the tomb or anything having to do with Jesus at this point, because they were sure he'd been killed by the Romans and were afraid that any one of them could be next.

It's only these two brave women who go to the tomb.

Do you know why they went?

They went not to greet a resurrected Lord, but to anoint a dead body for burial.

Now why would that be?

Why would those who followed him and listened to him and knew him by name, the men who left their boats and their families to go fish for people, the crowds who saw him give the blind their sight or multiply loaves and fishes, his closest disciples whom he told: "I will die, but will rise again," the women who knew he had raised their brother from the dead not have been waiting right outside his tomb on the third day to greet their resurrected Lord?

Why? It's because they, like so many of us, hold the power of God captive by our own minds, our own meager expectations, our own fear, and our own understanding of what is possible and what isn't. We get so good at thinking we know that we fail to take God at his word.

That is a strange thing to do.

It's strange, because it's not as though we don't have imaginations.

It's not as though we only act based on what is certain and sure.

Thomas Jefferson had faith enough to believe that 13 threadbare colonies could defeat the British Empire, which must have sounded impossible at the time. Not three weeks ago, our President declared that our churches would be full by Easter Sunday, though the experts told him it was impossible. Today, everyone guards themselves from a virus that they cannot see yet talk with them about the resurrected Lord and many are like the Disciple Thomas saying, "I've got to see it to believe." We don't have to see everything to believe, so I wonder, could it be that we are better at fear than faith?

Both fear and faith are based on what is not seen. Only we're so well-versed in worry and so uncomfortable with hope that people talk about a leap of faith rather than a leap of fear, as though being negative were any more material than optimism. Mark Twain once said, "I've had a lot of worries in my life, most of which never happened." I've hoped for a lot of things that never happened too, but still I worry, still, I fear.

I've been locked away in my house like those disciples, not expecting the moment when the anti-virus is discovered or the cure is found, but instead, preparing myself with a store of dried beans for the moment when it's no longer safe to even go to the grocery store. Here's my confession: I've been filling in the gaps of my knowledge with negative assumptions and pessimistic fairy tales. I do it even when I'm up here, in this pulpit. I can't hear you laugh, so there's a part of me that has assumed my jokes aren't funny.

Someone suggested we pipe in a laugh track like those old 80's sitcoms.

Maybe that would help?

I'm just kidding. That was a joke, but I can't tell whether or not you can tell that was a joke because I can't see your faces. I can't tell where my words are landing, and after preaching to this empty room for weeks, at some point in the sermon I assume you've wandered from the live stream to shop for toilet paper on *Amazon.com*. What's wrong with me? Because I'm out of the circle I assume I'm being left out, which is like thinking that because no one is coming over to the house, no one likes us anymore.

That doesn't make any sense, does it? So, I tell you, we can't just question our faith. We also must scrutinize our fears, for they're not rooted in facts, either.

We are not connected, but does a lack of connection feel the same as rejection?

When you don't have all the information, do you jump to conspiracy?

In a moment when you're not able to fulfill all your obligations, do you assume that they're not getting done? Do you imagine that if you're not there than no one will be?

The disciples didn't know where he was, so they assumed he was dead. The two Marys went to a tomb, spices in hand, to anoint a body for burial assuming they would find a corpse. When it wasn't there, they assumed someone had stolen it. When they felt the earthquake and saw an angel, they assumed they should be afraid. The assumptions are piling up now, yet a pile of assumptions doesn't equal a single fact. Why would we be people, who live our lives dismissing hope while acting on our fear, when all we really need to do is take God at his word? The angel told the two Marys: "He is not here; for he has been raised, as he said."

Too often we are these women, who at least are better than those disciples.

In this time of isolation and social distancing, who hasn't been afraid or downcast? What are we hoping for? What are we expecting? To anoint a body for burial. To get through another day. To scrape by, accept our lot, throw up our hands, give up and get used to it?

If you are erring on the side of the negative, I ask you: Did you hear the words of the Psalm? When Israel went out from Egypt they were met by the sea and assumed they were as good as dead, yet the sea fled before our God and they walked through on dry land.

*Why is it, O sea, that you flee?*

*It is because ours is the Lord,*

*whom the earth trembles before.*

Ours is the God who turns the rock into a pool of water. We must be bold to say that ours is the God who bridges gaps, set prisoners free, and works out His purpose in the midst of a viral pandemic. Just look. Look at the empty tomb. There we see that God, as God always does, gives us not the greatest gift that we can imagine, but the gift that God promised us, which is so glorious that we wouldn't dare imagine it.

Don't guess.

Don't fear.

Look into the tomb and see that he is not dead but risen. Notice the cloth thrown to the side, for up from slumber he rose to new life. And we will rise too.

We have to remember that.

He has risen that we might rise too.

If there is one word that we might use to describe this day, it is resurrection. Today is all about a resurrection hope, that when the sun sets on this strange season, a new day will dawn when we'll appreciate the chance to see people we love. Today we celebrate hope.

Hope, that when we don't have to be social distant, we'll strive for unity rather than division, and that rather than apathy, we will take on purpose.

Today, our lot is not despair, but joy, and we look forward to that time when we will no more take what we used to call normal for granted but will recognize every day as a gift and will count every moment precious. When I see your faces again, I don't know what I'll do, but because today is Easter, I know that I will see you.

I know that a new day will dawn.

How do I know it? For he is risen. He is risen indeed.

Alleluia.

Amen.

# The Lord is My Shepherd
1 Peter 2:19-25 and John 10:1-10

### Preached on May 3, 2020

Hearing Jesus talk about sheepfolds, gates, gatekeepers, and sheep stuck behind a wall hits a little close to home this morning. I wonder if the walls of your house started to feel like the walls of a prison? Have the locks that were installed to keep you safe started to feel like locks that keep you trapped inside? Have you been dying to get out, despite the dangers which lurk beyond the walls?

I've never thought much about getting a tattoo before, nor have I been much of a bowling enthusiast, but knowing that our Georgia governor has opened these places of business, as well as nail salons and barber shops, has made me excited about getting outside to do anything. Our kids on the other hand are happy just staying at home. Maybe your kids are happy, too. I've been hearing stories from parents of kids who act like they're living their best life, which has made me wonder about all kinds of things. Ours have been playing outside in this dinkey tree house I made them. They're eating lunch up there and acting like it's the coolest thing ever. They've also been going on walks with us and asking us to go with them when they ride their bikes. They've even been getting along with each other. All of this has made me wonder about the importance of all the junk which we've been filling their lives with.

In an effort to get the results that we're getting now, we signed them up for Cub Scouts, basketball, and softball. We sent them to camps and we drove them to lessons. We took them to movies, and we bought them expensive toys. So, why is it that they're so happy with a platform made from scrap lumber no more than two feet wide and four feet long, which I nailed up into a tree? Why is it that they're so happy making brownies with their mom in the kitchen? Why is it that they look forward to Friday nights when all we do is eat dinner while watching two episodes of *Gilmore Girls* together?

Could it be that what matters most to them is not what they get to do, but who they are doing these things with?

Could it be that more important than being entertained is feeling safe and heard and loved?

I'm coming to the realization in these days of quarantine that who is with us matters far more than what we're doing, and even more than where we are.

The Proverbs speak to this truth. Proverbs 21:9: *It is better to live on the roof than in the house shared by a contentious wife.*

Do you know that one?

I hope you're not living it.

I pray that your home life is safe and happy.

If it's not, then truly you are trapped, and many are. But if your kids are happy now, then take a lesson from them. I'm trying to. I'm trying to learn that what's beyond the gate is not as important as the one who stands guard over it. I'm trying to learn that there's a good reason to be wary of opening the gate too quickly, and we don't need to rush if we're rushing just to get out there. Now is the time to notice who is here.

There is one who watches over me and every member of this flock.

There is comfort which he brings in walking beside us all that must not be taken for granted, though that's what I too often do.

Our second scripture lesson from the Gospel of John speaks of one who is at the gate and who himself is the gate. It is Jesus Christ, the Good Shepherd, who promises to supply our every need. If you haven't missed a paycheck, then he's done it, and if you haven't given him thanks for such a miracle, then what have you been busy paying attention to?

That's what I want to preach about this morning.

The fact that I've been looking over the gate, longing to be some place other than where I am, longing to do some things that I'm not yet allowed to do to such a degree that I've been failing to notice the miracle of right here and right now.

Do you know what I'm talking about?

I'll give you an example: Last Tuesday was Lily's 11th birthday. That seems kind of sad, or it did seem sad to me. What does it mean to turn 11 if you can't have a party with your friends or even go out to your favorite restaurant? Knowing it would be different, my wife Sara worked hard to make the day special. She knew Lily wanted her bedroom redone, so Sara bought cute things to hang on the wall and a new bedspread and posters. Lily wanted all that to be a surprise. Subsequently, she volunteered to sleep in the guest room while we worked on it.

She asked us how long it would take to get her new room ready.

We told her, "Not too long."

"But aren't you taking down any walls?" she asked.

She's been watching a lot of *Fixer-upper*. Because of that, we worried her expectations might be a little too high. Only when she saw her room, she acted like we'd added a swimming pool or something. She smiled from ear to ear, as though her bedroom had been completely renovated. Then a neighbor brought by coffee cake for her breakfast, and another brought by cupcakes. She opened birthday cards and received phone calls. With chalk, the kids across the street wrote, "Happy Birthday Lily" in the middle of the road. Friends from school drove by in a birthday parade. Then, right around lunch a man walked by, noticed the chalk writing in the road, and asked Lily if she would like for him to come by later and play "Happy Birthday" on his trombone. It was funny when she walked inside and said, "Mama, some man just offered to come by later and play his trombone." We didn't know whether to be excited or suspicious, only then it turned out to be Bob Scarr, who many of you know. Right at 5:30, after she had talked with all her grandparents, Bob Scarr drove over with his wife and played Lily "Happy Birthday" in the middle of the road. After that, some cake, and a small-scale fireworks display, Lily told us it was the best birthday she'd ever had.

Why? Because within these gates she's loved, and she knows it.

Within these gates, she's cared for.

Within these gates she knows she's precious, and the difference between children like her and too many of their parents is that they children still know that's all anyone needs.

The rest of us are thinking: "But, there's bigger and better! For your birthday we can take you to White Water or Six Flags." What's so funny is that I've seen kids have more fun in puddles lately than they ever would have at White Water, so the question becomes: Who have we been taking them there for? Who convinced us that we need so much more than what we have already?

There is only one Good Shepherd, but so many try to lead us, don't they? Yet, we don't have to work as hard as they say we do to find joy, do we?

When the dust settles from our busy lives, are there not blue skies to be seen overhead?

When we can't go anywhere, don't we realize that we have so much of what we've been looking for?

Sometimes it's only after I've grown exhausted looking for answers and fulfilment that I look up to see that God has always been right there. I just keep looking past God. While I've been searching, God has been waiting for me to notice that God's always been there, right by my side. The Lord is my shepherd, and even though I walk through the darkest valley, I fear no evil.

Why? For God is with me.

We have to get better at noticing that.

We must all get better at seeing God as God stands at the gate, watches over God's sheep, and leads the flock. To do that I must stop looking over the hills into tomorrow, because God is present to us here today.

It's like we're waiting for something to happen, without realizing what's actually happening.

We must stop waiting for things to change back to normal, to notice that even if normal never comes, the Lord has not abandoned us.

It's in a moment such as this one when we can open our eyes to see that, still, mercy follows me. Still, he anoints my head with oil.

Still, my cup overflows.

Our own Chick Freud sent us pastors a TED talk, a speech given by a *National Geographic* photographer and he described his job like this:

*I always knew that just beyond the rat race was incredible beauty.*

*My job was to see that, to take a picture of that.*

*To not fail to see the beauty that is always there.*

What I want you to hear today are the words of the Apostle Paul: that with our current suffering is glory being revealed to us. In the midst of all this loss are gifts we are fools to take for granted. Even in the presence of death and trauma are moments of undeniable beauty. Something that has brought tears to my eyes every time I've thought about it is how many are having to say goodbye to their grandmothers, fathers, or mothers through a mask in the best circumstances, and over the phone in the worst. Death still comes in many forms while all our attention is on one particular virus.

Matt Burnham's father was rushed to Emory hospital after a major stroke. He was then transferred to hospice. While the family waited, they played his favorite hymn, "It is well with my soul." I won't sing it for you, but I want to just read you the second verse:

*Though Satan should buffet,*

*though trials should come,*

*let this blest assurance control,*

*that Christ has regarded my helpless estate,*

*and hath shed his own blood for my soul.*

My friends, there have been many tribulations and trials though the eras of human history, and faith will sustain us through this one. Remember that there are many highs and lows in this life, and through all the lows God has walked beside us. Know it now, as it has always been. In this moment, in this time, it is well, because God is with us, just as God promised.

Amen.

# How Can We Know the Way?
## 1 Peter 2:2-10 and John 14:1-14

### Preached on May 10, 2020

LAST WEEK I was listening to a radio show that comes on National Public Radio called *This American Life*. The show reports on the lives of Americans, 10 to 12 minutes each. In recent weeks, the stories have mostly been from people in New York City: sick parents trying to care for their children in the confines of their apartments or overwhelmed ambulance drivers, sometimes able to do little more than nothing for the dying and always afraid that they themselves will contract the virus. Last week the subject was lighter, but still COVID-19-related. In honor of all those high school seniors who are having to miss their prom or settle for a virtual prom, *This American Life* spent the entire hour celebrating what for many is an important milestone - what for others is a source of dread or embarrassment.

This prom-themed episode included stories from tuxedo rental staff who reported on the state of returned tuxedo rentals. There was one story of a high school class in the Midwest who safely danced in the basement of the school gym while a tornado swept through town, others of young men stood up by their dates, mothers who made their daughters uncomfortable with their advice, and post-prom high school seniors who had spent all this time and effort looking forward to a night that failed to meet their expectations.

The whole show brought back memories for me of my own senior prom. I remember the weeks leading up to it. It seemed so daunting. I had to rent a tuxedo, make dinner reservations at *Ruth's Chris Steakhouse*, buy tickets, order a corsage, and most nerve-racking of all, find a date. Remembering my personal experience with prom, I realized how I would feel if my senior prom were canceled due to a global pandemic: relieved. I would have felt completely and dramatically relieved to not have to go through the dauntingly-vulnerable process which leads up to a night that I'll always remember, not because it was particularly magical, but because it stretched me in ways that the academics of high school never could.

My prom memories include how I finally asked a girl on a date I had been wanting to ask on a date for years. We danced and we talked. I almost kissed her but lost my nerve.

Why? Because going into uncharted territory without knowing what's going to happen next is terrifying, especially if you're the kind of person who's afraid to ask for advice or directions. That's why I admire Thomas.

He's pretty much my favorite disciple, because he is always brave enough to ask.

In that passage I just read he says to Jesus, "Lord, we do not know where you are going. How can we know the way?"

I've never heard of that being a memory verse, but it ought to be. With life always stretching us and pushing us into the unknown, asking for directions is absolutely imperative.

I've said it before. We call him Doubting Thomas, but truly, he's just the one who is brave enough to speak his doubts out loud. Every one of them was thinking or feeling the same thing, they just weren't willing to say it. Had the Disciples been driving in a car, lost at night on the highway, Thomas would have been the one who walked into the dimly lit gas station to ask for directions. Had the Disciples been students all lost in Spanish class, Thomas would have been the one to ask the teacher to go over the verbs she'd just conjugated a second time. Had the Disciples all been young high school seniors, nervous about asking a girl to the senior prom, Thomas would have been the one who called his older brother to say, "There's a girl I really want to ask, but where do I even start?"

Some of us pretend that we're doing fine or that we know our way through unchartered waters but take note of Thomas' example: It's ok to ask for directions. It's ok. For the truth is, no one makes it though unchartered waters without help.

A pastor named Shannon Michael Pater wrote about our passage from the Gospel of John saying that the role Jesus plays and which he calls all his disciples to play in moments such as this one is like that of a midwife and a hospice chaplain. Both of these roles stand in between two very different realities. Both these roles perform a pivotal task during a dramatic transition. Both these roles boldly proclaim: Maybe there is pain right now, but it's the pain of in-between.

Something is happening now.

Something is changing.

One chapter will come to an end, but another will begin.

Just relax, if you can, and wait.

That's not easy to do. What's easier is just to do something. Anything.

One of the most stressful feelings I can think of is that of being late for a meeting or appointment. That feeling that comes from knowing that I'm supposed to be somewhere, only I'm not there. I'm stuck in traffic, I'm lost, or I'm trying to politely exit a conversation. Worse, is that feeling of knowing I'm supposed to be somewhere, only I can't remember where. Whatever it is, there's severe anxiety that comes with knowing that I'm in the wrong place, that I'm supposed to be someplace other than where I am. Do you know the feeling?

Today, that's the feeling that I pretty much feel all the time.

I always feel like there's something happening that I'm supposed to be at. I wake up already feeling like I'm running behind. I have to constantly remind myself that still, most things are closed and besides that, this is a time for waiting, only waiting is uncomfortable and it's hard. I'd much rather have a timeline or a road map so I could know where it is that we're going and how long it's going to take to get there.

Do you know what I mean?

The shelter-in-place orders are lifting, but to what are we returning? Some hope we're getting back to normal, only sitting in a restaurant with half the tables roped off doesn't seem normal. Waiting in line outside a Home Depot doesn't seem normal. How long is all this going to last? What does the future hold? How do we get there? Those are the questions Thomas was asking. Again, I like Thomas. He's always brave enough to ask the questions that everyone else is afraid to ask. Jesus tells his disciples, "Don't let your hearts be troubled… In my Father's house there are many dwelling places" and I'm going there to prepare a place for you.

"That sounds great Jesus," Thomas says, "But how do we get there?"

I love that.

He just says it: "Actually, no, we have no idea where you are going. We barely understand what you're talking about. How can we know the way?"

It's like Jesus assumes that we're capable of remaining calm at a time like this.

It's like he thinks we ought to just be able to follow him as sheep follow a shepherd.

Doesn't he know how anxious and afraid we all are?

I don't like this. Do you?

I'll gladly wear my cloth facemask to the grocery store for another month if it means I won't have to wear it once June comes.

The part that scares me now is the not knowing. What's the world going to look like this Fall? What's going to happen next? I know that ultimately there is a place prepared for you and me in the Kingdom of God, but there are a few steps to take between here and there so, like Thomas, I'd like a slightly more detailed plan than the one Jesus has mapped out. Unfortunately, there's no map in the second scripture lesson. Instead, there's this assurance: "Believe me because of the works themselves."

That's what Jesus says in response to Phillip, who wants to see the Father.

Jesus says, "Who do you think I am?"

Then to Thomas, as if to say, "I've been leading you by the hand this whole time. What makes you think I'm going to stop now?"

I want you to know that your church is doing all kinds of things as we step into this unchartered territory. Your congregation's elected representatives are meeting weekly, some nearly daily. Councils and committees are working together, they're moving quickly, we're learning from regional and national leaders in the Presbyterian Church, we're meeting with other area church leaders comparing notes, we're reading what the governor and school system are thinking. But what I believe is most helpful, which only a church like this one can do, is to remember that God hasn't failed us yet, so why be afraid that God's going to fail us now?

"Believe me, because of the works themselves," Jesus said. And what were those works?

He healed the sick.

He fed the hungry.

He encouraged the hopeless.

He relieved heavy burdens.

He gave us his very body and blood.

He was the incarnation of the living God who, when the Hebrew people heard the Egyptian horde behind them and saw the sea before them, divided the water on each side giving Moses and the people a dry path to deliver them.

When they reached the other side Moses' sister Miriam sang, "Sing to the Lord, for he has triumphed gloriously. Horse and rides he has thrown into the sea." Those words were sung and repeated then written down. Why? Because there have been other seas to cross, other hopeless situations to be delivered from, so we must remember that God has been leading us through the unknown since the dawn of time with no intention of relenting until we reach the Promised Land. Jesus said to the disciples: "In my father's house, there are many dwelling places. If it were not so, would I have told you that I go to prepare a place for you."

"How can we know that we'll get there?" we all ask.

Therefore, we must remember, it's because God has led us this far.

God knit us together in our mother's womb when the womb was all we knew.

In our mother's arms God filled our lungs with breath, knowing already the number of hairs on our heads.

God watched as we stood and took our first steps.

God heard us cry as we fell.

God wiped those tears from our eyes.

Not far. God was close, as one chapter closed and the next one began.

On this Mother's Day we give thanks to God for our mothers, and we rejoice that, like a mother, our God has been our ever-present help in times of transition, promising that God will not drop us and will be waiting for us on the other side of everything.

It reminds me of my own mother.

She didn't go to her senior prom. She considered herself too mature at the time, and she insisted that I go to mine.

"But who will I ask? What will I say?" Those were my questions, but I'm not sure I had to ask them. She was there to help me. One thing I remember her saying is, "If I had any idea how scared 18-year-old boys were of 18-year-old girls I would have been a much more confident 18-year-old girl." Through every transition of my life, from birth to high school graduation, marriage and our first and second child, I've been blessed to benefit from those who have been through it already and, holding my hand, have testified that it's going to be OK.

Certainly, we are in the midst of another terrifying transition, but who is with us in it?

Miriam, who pointed to God's hand dividing the sea.

Thomas, who knew who to ask for directions.

This month I've been reading about Churchill who faced the Blitz. When German bombers flew over London in the middle of the night, he'd go to the roof, still in his nightgown, helmet on his head, believing death was better than surrender. Then I consider the history of this church, with the likes of Pastor Palmer, who returned to our sanctuary seeing a floor covered in the blood of wounded confederates and union soldiers alike, the pews burned to fuel fires, and the congregation terrified, isolated, and not knowing where to go next. To whom did he testify? From whom did he ask for directions?

Our church came back from that and we will make it through this too. Step by step we will do it, following Christ who leads from where we are now to where we will be – God's house with a place for you, a place for me.

Alleluia.

Amen.

# I Will Not Leave You Orphaned
## 1 Peter 3:13-22 and John 14:15-21

### Preached on May 17, 2020

A FORMATIVE moment in my life happened during the Great Recession of 2008. I was serving my first church in Lilburn, as an associate pastor. The senior pastor had just left for a church in Florida, so attendance was already dropping, as were the finances. Certainly, the economic forecast didn't help the financial situation, so the Session met and one of the first things they did was allow the Interim Pastor's contract to expire. They didn't renew it. They couldn't afford to. Suddenly, I was the only pastor at that church.

This was a problem, because I didn't know what I was doing.

When the Finance Committee reported how badly they projected the budget deficit to be, I was terrified. I don't remember sleeping much the night after that meeting. The next day I went to the Presbytery office. In a sense, that's the church's governing body, and there I spoke with the Executive Presbyter (an impressive title for an impressive man). I didn't have an appointment, but he saw me anyway. Perhaps the receptionist could see the terror on my face. I told him how bad the projected budget deficit was, and that I feared this church might close its doors.

"What should I do?" I asked him.

He took the situation seriously, then he took me seriously asking, "How much do you know about finances Joe?"

I told him that I'd never successfully managed my checkbook.

Then he said, "What makes you think that you're the one to do anything?"

This was one of the most important questions I've ever been asked.

"What makes you think that you're the one to do anything?"

"What makes me think that I'm the one to do anything? Well, who else is there?"

I didn't ask him that out loud, but that's what I was thinking. Before I had a chance to ask, he said, "Are there business owners in the congregation? Bankers? Accountants? Get them together and make sure they know the situation. Ask them for help." As he gave me this advice, he didn't use Jesus' words, exactly, but it was close enough. Through this man, I could hear Christ saying to me as he said to his disciples so long ago:

*I will not leave you orphaned.*

*You are not all on your own.*

*When you pass through the waters, they may rise, but I will be with you.*

*And through the rivers, they shall not overwhelm you.*

*When you walk through fire you shall not be burned, and the flame shall not consume you.*

Such are the promises of Scripture and this is the story of my life as a pastor. Every time I was brave enough to ask for help, my shepherd has supplied my need. Every time I boldly took inventory of the limit of my ability, God stood beside me in the breach. Every time I faced what seemed insurmountable, every time I was told not to rely on my own strength, every time I wondered, "But how will I find the words?" "How will I do it?" "How will I face the grief or the terror or the death again," a touch of the hand or a word spoken in love reminded me that I am not alone.

Coleen and Cheryl sang it, didn't they?

*I believe in the sun even when it's not shining.*
*I believe in love even when I don't feel it.*
*I believe in God even when God is silent.*

"I will not leave you orphaned," Jesus promised.

Maybe he didn't promise that it would be easy.

Maybe he didn't promise that we'd always sleep through the night.

But what he did promise was that he'd be there even when the world can't see him.

"You know him, because he abides with you, and he will be in you."

Now that's a promise.

It's a promise like the one in the song, which was written during the Holocaust and was found after, on a slip of paper. Who wrote it? And how did she become so enlightened? I don't know, but I do know that she was right. The sun is there even when it's not shining. Love is real, even when I don't feel it. God is here even if we can't hear God, and sometimes it takes a concentration camp to teach us such a lesson. Or sometimes it takes a viral pandemic.

This is a time when many are reaching the end of their rope.

Isolation is getting the best of some of us.

Fear is wearing us down.

Paranoia is creeping into our minds, prompting us to ask hard questions in a time without easy answers.

I've felt fear, worry, frustration and anger. Only, who should I be angry with? We look for a villain, someone to blame; yet perhaps the thing that will bring us hope is looking not for the villains, but for the helpers.

One of the great Presbyterian ministers of history, Mr. Rogers, was bold to confess:

*When I was a boy and I would see scary things in the news, my mother would say to me, 'Look for the helpers. You will always find people who are helping.' To this day, especially in times of "disaster," I always remember my mother's words and I am always comforted by realizing that there are still so many helpers – so many caring people in this world.*

He's right. There are many helpers, but can you see them? Christ promised, "I will not leave your orphaned," but do you perceive it? I was reminded this week of a story I've told you before of a woman I went to visit. She was upset with the church. Upset with life, really, and because I was there, she let me have it: "At that church of yours, pastor, no one speaks to me. I've been gone for four weeks and no one has noticed."

I hate hearing that kind of thing.

It breaks my heart, because I know it's true.

It happens.

Sometimes the church isn't there when we need our family of faith the most. Only, in that moment, her phone rang. It was Gloria from the church, calling just to say to this woman, "I haven't seen you and I've missed you. How have you been?" The conversation lasted just a few seconds. The woman I was visiting said something like, "Gloria, thank you for calling. But Joe, our pastor is here, and I was just telling him something. Thank you for calling. Goodbye." Then she looked to me, "Where was I? Oh yes, no one from that church ever calls me!"

What is it that clouds our vision to the helpers, even when they are there, right before our eyes? "I will not leave you orphaned" he said to the disciples. Like this woman, they couldn't see it always. Peter didn't believe anyone could save him once Christ was arrested, so rather than call for help or react in faith, out of self-reliance and self-preservation he denied him three times. Or consider Judas who betrayed him. A wise man once asked me, "Would Christ have forgiven Judas had he repented?" Of course. He forgave everyone, all of humanity, hanging there on the cross saying, "Forgive them Father, for they know not what they do." Still, consider how often we focus on what is broken within us, rather than the grace he provides. How often do we focus on what is broken in the world, rather than God's love at work in helpers great and small? How often do we depend on ourselves, not believing in forgiveness, really, just holding it in, letting the darkness in our hearts fester rather than inviting love's light to cast it out.

Of course, asking for this kind of help is hard to do so.

Seeing it is hard to do.

Faith is required.

It reminds me of the third Indiana Jones movie, *Indiana Jones and the Last Crusade*. Apparently, Indiana Jones 5 is coming out in 2022. I heard that in this one, instead of a whip, Harrison Ford has a walker. I'm just kidding. Even if it's bad I'll probably still go see it. All through fourth- and fifth grade I wore a fedora to school, I was such a big fan of Indiana Jones. The greatest of the series is the third movie: *Indiana Jones and the Last Crusade*. In that one, there's this incredible scene. A deep chasm stands in the hero's way. It's so deep he can't see the bottom. It's too wide to jump. There's nothing for him to catch with his whip to swing across. The ancient manuscript tells him the only thing he can do is take a step into the nothing with enough faith to know that he won't fall.

So, that's what he does.

With a sweaty forehead and a body trembling he steps out and his foot finds a bridge. He couldn't see the bridge, but it was there. He took the first step then kept going and reaching the other side he looked back, and it was clear that an invisible bridge had been there the whole time. We can't always see to know that he will not leave us orphaned, but I tell you, once this is all over, we will be able to look back on this time knowing that his hand has been moving all along. We just couldn't see it.

I know that, because that's how it is.

Faith is easier in retrospect, just as our hindsight is 20/20. So, as I look back on the years of my life, I see it, while in the moment I wasn't sure. I didn't know that the church I served in Lilburn would go from a projected budget deficit to end the year with a surplus. The first time someone asked me how I did it sarcastically I said, "Well, I'm a financial genius." Sarcastically, because that wasn't true.

God's hand was at work, and while I wasn't always sure where we were going or whether or not we were doing the right thing, He was leading us, nonetheless. Likewise, it was a strange thing to ask of you about two years ago to invest in new cameras so that we could worship over the internet. Can you imagine where we'd be, had wise leaders in our church not encouraged us in this direction? Then, about three years ago today I was telling the church I served in Tennessee that I'd accepted a call to serve a church in Marietta, Georgia. I uprooted my family. We left people we love. While today I see God's hand guiding us, in the moment, I felt like Indiana Jones, stepping into the great unknown.

Of course, it was not unknown. It never is.

I was not alone, because we never are.

Open your eyes to see that he is with you where you are today, at work in your life, changing things for the better, and be prepared to reach out for help. There is no need to rely on yourself, for he has not left you nor I orphaned. So, let us step into our unknown future with faith, trusting God's promise that God will be with us always, even to the end of the age.

Amen.

# The God of Love and Peace Will Be with You
## Genesis 1:1-4 and 2nd Corinthians 13:11-13

### Preached on June 5, 2020

ONE MORNING the week before last I was walking our dogs around the block. I wasn't exactly happy to be doing that, but it's an important thing to do. Since being stuck inside our home all day myself, I have new sympathy for what their lives are like, so maybe it was more of an obligation than a joy to greet the morning by slowly walking around the block while our dogs smell every mailbox, stump, and branch, then dutifully picking up whatever they leave behind.

About halfway around the block, a woman hauling limbs from her front yard to the curb said something to me which changed the way I greeted that new day. I missed it the first time she said it, so I stopped, took my headphones out, to hear her say it again, "This is the day that the Lord has made!"

Do you know that feeling of being stuck in an obligation or to be simply moving through the steps and all at once your eyes are open to how lucky you are? This was the perfect thing to hear someone say that morning. For one thing it reminded me that this was the day that the Lord has made. It was a beautiful morning, and it was gift. It also evoked my awareness of the divine moving around us. But most of all it was so nice to hear someone say something that I knew exactly how to respond to.

With a smile on my face I responded to this woman's, "This is the day that the Lord has made," with my, "Let us rejoice and be glad in it!" Yet how many other times is it not nearly so easy to know what to say?

I remember vividly standing in the foyer of our old house in Tennessee just a few years ago. Our two little girls stopping me in my tracks to ask, "I know that when we were tiny babies we were inside Mama's tummy, but how did we get out?" Worse than that, have your children or grandchildren asked about the events of the past two weeks?

The protests?

Did they ask you if it was true that as George Floyd died, he called for his mother?

Did they have trouble understanding why the police, who have answered that high call to help and service, had a knee on Mr. Floyd's neck?

Why they stood idly by as he said, "I can't breathe"?

Were they scared when they saw the damage done to the CNN Center just down I-75?

What did the children of police officers think, if they witnessed the video of squad cars burning?

Or what did the parents of protestors think when they read the tweet: "When looting starts the shooting starts"?

To me, it was equally difficult to make sense of that image of our President, standing in front of a church he doesn't attend, holding up a Bible.

This is a time where I have asked myself that most difficult of questions: Where is God at work in all of this?

What are we to say to anyone, much less our kids, as they make sense out a world that all of us are having trouble making any sense of ourselves?

An old friend of mine, Rev. Amos Disasa sat his son down to talk about race. Amos serves First Presbyterian Church in Dallas, Texas as their Senior Pastor. The two of us have a lot in common, though we don't look alike. He was born in Ethiopia to Ethiopian parents, so race has played a subtle part in our friendship since we were classmates at Presbyterian College. Just after seminary the two of us spent several days in Montreat, North Carolina, for a conference of Presbyterian ministers. One night we went out for a beer at a bar called the *Town Pump*. Immediately, upon sitting down, it became obvious to me that this was a bar for locals, not out of town Presbyterian ministers, so I said to Amos, "I feel a little out of place." Amos said to me, "Joe, do you see anyone else from Ethiopia in here?"

Amos married a white woman from West Virginia.

Their two children are of mixed race.

Last Thursday Amos told the congregation of First Presbyterian in Dallas that in light of recent events he sat his 10-year-old son down to explain what's been happening and what it means for him as a male with dark skin.

"Your skin color will make some people uncomfortable. Some people will see your body as a threat," he told his son.

Then, thinking about George Floyd, Ahmaud Arbery, or any number of other unarmed Black men who have been killed recently, his son asked, "Can that happen to me?"

His father said, "Yes."

Then, his son's second question was, "Can that happen to you?"

Again, his father said, "Yes."

Our children have asked me many difficult questions, but "Where do babies come from?" doesn't come close to either of these. Among all the many difficult questions our children have asked me, they've never asked me to answer a question that I would have been this sad to answer truthfully as these two questions, but we all must say something about the events of the last two weeks. Only, where do we even begin?

I wonder if where we ought to begin is with the words of our Declaration of Independence:

*We hold these truths to be self-evident, that all men are created equal.*

Or with those words which have marked the beginning of each school day for my children and your children:

*I pledge allegiance to the Flag of the United States of America, and to the Republic for which it stands, one Nation under God, indivisible, with liberty and justice for all.*

Or those words which lady liberty holds precious shielding Ellis Island:

*Give me your tired, your poor, your huddled masses yearning to breathe free.*

*The wretched refuse of your teeming shore.*

*Send these, the homeless, tempest-tossed to me,*

*I lift my lamp beside the golden door.*

Or with the dream Dr. King preached about 57 years ago before the Lincoln Monument:

*I have a dream that one day on the red hills of Georgia sons of former slaves and the sons of former slave-owners will be able to sit down together at the table of brotherhood.*

Even in these moments when the table of brotherhood has erupted in protests and riots with shielded police facing off with the crowds as democrats and republicans prove that truly anything can be made into a political issue, we turn to these words to remind us of who we're intending to be. We turn to these words to remember again, that even if they don't describe where we are, they do describe where we are going. Then we turn to the words of Scripture to remind us of who is with us on our journey.

In our first scripture lesson, God spoke our world into existence. Some people think that these verses are trying to replace the Science text books, but I say they are trying to remind us of the power of our words.

God spoke our world into existence.

My friends, if we don't like the way our world looks today, then know that our words have the power to create a new reality. So, we must remember again those words which gave birth to our nation and stand against those words which might take it all away and the violence that would burn it all down.

Violence is how we lose ourselves, while words, beautiful words are how we find our way back. The words of Scripture testify to the reality that hovering over a formless void was the wind from God which swept over the face of the waters. When God spoke light into that darkness and as the Spirit swirled the waters of chaos into order, God spoke again saying that it was good. Don't forget that God still does.

God hasn't given up on God's creation.

Neither can we, and God calls us to show the indifferent, the prejudiced, the polarizing, the power drunk, that a more ideal union is possible, that justice will roll down like waters and righteousness like an ever-flowing stream.

The Apostle Paul ends his second letter to the Church in Corinth saying,

*Finally, brothers and sisters, farewell. Put things in order, listen to my appeal, agree with one another, live in peace, and the God of love and peace will be with you. Greet one another with a holy kiss. All the saints greet you. The grace of the Lord Jesus Christ, the love of God, and the communion of the Holy Spirit be with all of you.*

This is a powerful way to end a letter.

It's a call to order and harmony.

It's a call to love.

It's a reminder to recognize God at work in our midst.

Also, it is likely his great goodbye.

How do we honor his memory, or the memory of any of God's saints, if rather than agree with one another, we make our brothers and sisters our enemies?

How do we follow the model of any who have loved us if we stop working for peace?

How do we honor the memory of those who spilled their blood for the ideals of this nation if we turn to tyranny and chaos, rather than love and the communion of the Holy Spirit?

As Americans and as Christians, our persistent charge is to join the God of creation in forming a more perfect union, a more noble brotherhood, to continue on in the building of that city on a hill where all are valued, all are honored, and where all so truly matter.

Let us never ignore the brokenness.

Let us never silence the angry, saying peace, peace, when there is no peace.

Instead, let us listen to the lady who called me to recognize that this is the day that the Lord has made. Today, let us pray, let us listen, let us walk, let us dance, let us work for something better for our children. But above all else, let us rejoice and be glad in this world our God is still creating, sustaining, and redeeming.

Alleluia.

Amen.

# The Beginning of the Good News of Jesus Christ, the Son of God
## Psalm 91:9-12 and Mark 1:1-20

**Preached on June 14, 2020**

THIS IS a strange time for me as a preacher. I say that not hoping for sympathy, but because what I'm feeling now may be something close to what you're feeling. Maybe like you, my relationships feel like they're suffering because without seeing people I care about, physically, I can't really tell where things stand, and I fill in what I don't know with too much negative stuff. They say most of communication is nonverbal. That's why phone calls are imperfect, and emails are even worse.

We understand and process between words, which we hear, with what we see. If we see them smile back at us, we know they're happy. Or by watching as tears well up in their eyes, we know more about what they're feeling than words could ever tell us. Plus, we feel close to people when they touch us. We know we're being understood based on all kinds of cues. But I'm here in this pulpit doing a lot of talking, only I'm talking without knowing how what I'm saying is being received.

You might know how strange that is, or how less-than-ideal it is.

What I typically do as I preach is look at your faces. Doing so, I can often tell when I've gone on for too long because someone has fallen asleep. I can tell when I've gone too far or not far enough because I'm reading your faces while I'm talking.

You do the same thing.

I wonder if the thing we all are missing most is face-to-face interaction. I miss it at the grocery store because I can't tell if people are smiling beneath their masks. You might miss face-to-face interaction with grandchildren or face-to-face interaction with our church family. It's is a human need and, so, that's what God gives us in this long Scripture passage from the Gospel of Mark.

Rev. Cassie Waits and I are the preachers for this month and next. She suggested we focus on the Gospel of Mark and this is the first in a series six. These are six sermons, six readings from the Gospel of Mark, covering about the first half of this Gospel. We'll cover a lot ground in these next several weeks, as we just did today. The Scripture lesson began with a clear title: The beginning of the good news of Jesus Christ, the Son of God.

What we all know about Jesus is that he is God in flesh in blood, walking around, moving into our neighborhood, taking on the mortal coil, experiencing our joys and fears, and even suffering. He's not a bystander to human existence; rather, in Christ, our God takes human flesh. I don't want to rush past this miracle, though I know you've heard all about it many times before, because it's just so earth-shattering and nearly unprecedented.

There's just not much else like it in the world of religion.

Much of what we know of the religion of the ancient Greeks is quite different. Did you ever see those old Greek myth movies like *Jason and the Argonauts*? They're movies with a bunch of guys in beards and animal skins fighting off clay-mation monsters. The way I remember it, just as in the ancient myths, the gods in those movies had this place up in the clouds on Mt. Olympus and they could look down on the earth to watch the human dramas unfold.

According to the myths, occasionally they'd come down, but what sticks with me from the movies was this portal that they had to look into our lives.

It was like their TV.

It was reality TV before there was reality TV.

Their window into our lives was on the floor. They moved the clouds to watch and be entertained, but how much could they really know of humans when watching from a distance? How much can anyone really know about anything when watching from a distance? So, what does God do? God comes close.

From the Gospel of Mark, we know that Jesus was the incarnate God in human form, walking the earth in our shoes.

Do you remember other stories inspired by this kind of incarnation?

There's the *Prince and the Pauper,* where these two boys who look alike switch places. The prince finds out how hard it is to be a pauper and the pauper finds out that being the prince isn't all about sitting around eating cake. They're both better for it.

Why? Because when assumptions drive us, we get all messed up.

A couple of older gentlemen back in Tennessee once told me about the first time they met a Yankee. When they were just young boys, having never met one before, they threw rocks at him. Now, why would someone do that? How could someone do that? But when we don't see people, we make stuff up, and what we make up is nearly all the time far worse than the truth.

These two probably thought he had come to town like the carpet baggers they'd heard about from their parents and grandparents. Imagine if we based all our impressions of people not on what we learned after meeting them, but on what we'd heard.

I went to college with a Tennessean named Will who went to school up in Maine. The first people he met up there were surprised he wore shoes. Why? Because if your opinion of people from east Tennessee is based on the *Beverly Hillbillies*, you'll think all kinds of crazy stuff. So, what does God do?

Does God take someone's word for it?

Does God come to understand the human condition, based on what God can see through the clouds?

No.

Again, and again, God draws near.

God draws near to get to know us, and we must constantly allow our assumptions to die, lest we see the world as full of enemies rather than brothers and sisters.

After the girls are in bed, Sara and I watch TV together. Right now, we're watching a show called *Poldark*. It's one of those Masterpiece Classics that comes on PBS like *Downton Abby*. I find some of the Masterpiece shows to be a little slow, but *Poldark* has put me to sleep just a couple times. The main character in this show is a British veteran of the American Revolution. This redcoat goes home to Cornwall to manage his family's copper mine, and he gets into all these adventures. He's like an 18th Century Rambo with a British accent, exceptional manners, and an enlightened mind. On the subject of war, Poldark tells his wife, "It's horrible what men can do to other men once they've convinced themselves that their enemy is less than human."

I think about how police officers are being talked about today.

Now I do stand with those who march peacefully, knowing that some bad officers have treated those in their care as less than human. And I don't just know it, I've seen it. However, any crowd or politician who's been convinced that all police officers are evil are promoting the same prejudice they're protesting against.

It's horrible what people will do to each other once they've convinced themselves that their enemy or opponent or subject or family member is less than human.

What if we all took the time to say to ourselves in the midst of our anger or frustration, "I don't agree with this person - this liberal, this conservative, this protestor, this police officer - and I wonder why they think the way they do." What we all too often do, instead, is assume we already know, saying to ourselves, "Oh, I know. They must be stupid. Or bad." What's different about Jesus is this: He could have sat up in the clouds making assumptions; instead, he took on our flesh to really understand. He just kept drawing closer and closer to us until he understood why we are all so broken and confused. Because he understood us all, and why we do the things that we do, even from the cross he called out, "Forgive them father for they know not what they do."

In this Scripture lesson from the Gospel of Mark he even got baptized.

Why? For what?

What sins did the Lord need to have washed away? But that's not the point. He's taking on our condition. He's baptized to be as we are and to do as we have. He just keeps coming closer and closer. He didn't even keep his distance from Satan.

Now that's important, isn't it?

Unlike Matthew and Luke, Mark doesn't include any details of what this encounter was like. Typically, I would say that being in the wilderness for forty days and tempted by Satan sounds graphic enough, but after three months of isolation we might say: Forty days? That's nothing!

Still, consider what happens to us after forty days or three weeks of isolation.

What has happened to us after three weeks of only looking out on the world through our television screen or Facebook feed.

Consider what happens to our view of the world when we aren't a part of it?

Consider what happens to how we think about people when we can't see them or hear them or be with them face-to-face.

How hard it is to get to know a person through email.

How hard it is to ease a troubled relationship or work out a disagreement if you can't see their faces and really understand.

For the past three months, we may as well have been up in the clouds, looking down, having no real understanding of the people we're looking down on. When that's the case it becomes all too easy to give up. Yet, Cindy Buchanan (member of our church and mother of my oldest friend, Matt) said it better than anyone: "The Zombie movies convinced us that after months of a viral pandemic we'd all be eating each other. Only, when I actually see people, I see how much kindness there is in the world."

The tempter whispers in our ears to just give up on people who think differently than we do. But Jesus never did that. Even after 40 days in the wilderness, tempted by Satan himself, Jesus never gave up on us.

After the temptation, our Scripture lesson's last few verses described what he was doing. John had been arrested and he started proclaiming good news. Then, he passed along the Sea of Galilee.

That's all it says: "He passed along."

What do you think that means?

I imagine he was whistling.

Or that he was enjoying the waves as they hit his feet.

Then he looked up and saw two fishermen, Simon and his brother Andrew. They were casting a net into the sea, for they were fishermen.

"Follow me and I will make you fish for people," he said to them. And immediately they left their nets and followed him.

A few years ago, I got caught reading the Bible in a doctor's waiting room. A man said to me, "I love to read the Bible too. It tells us what God is like and how we should be."

What is God like? God is like Jesus. Longing to know us. Always loving us. Saving all his harsh words for those religious authorities who cared more about rules and status than people. And how should we be? Not like them. Like him.

Amen.

# A Vaccine Is Not Enough to Save Us
Psalm 103:6-14 and Mark 2:1-22

### Preached on June 21, 2020

THAT WAS 22 whole verses I just read. It seemed like a long reading to me, because I'm used to dealing with reading only a few verses at a time. Generally, I read maybe half that many, so that my sermons are based on just one moment in Scripture rather than a chain of events. The benefit of basing a sermon on just a few verses or on one particular event in Scripture is that I can focus on just one thing. Like most husbands, that's better for me.

Because it's impossible for me to multitask, I just focus on one thing at a time, like one event in the life of Jesus or one small section of his teachings. But when we read several verses describing several moments in the life of Christ as we just did, it's possible to see significant similarities as Jesus moves from one healing to the next, and then to a statement about patches on clothes and new wine in old wineskins. Reading all these 22 verses at once, I see how the whole series of events works together, and for the first time I noticed the similarities between the healing of the paralytic in the first 12 verses of our reading and the healing of Levi in the next five.

However, our Bible doesn't call it the healing of Levi.

The heading in my Bible has: "Jesus heals a paralytic" over verses 1-12 and "Jesus calls Levi" over verses 13-17. What I want to focus on this morning is how Jesus deals with both of these men in a similar way, though we may think of them differently. While maybe we call one of these events a "healing" and the other a "calling", Jesus deals with them both the same way: By forgiving their sins.

Just that commonality may have something important to teach us about the way Christ is at work in the world. We mostly think of sin and sickness as two different things. We go one place to be healed from a physical issue and another for the kind of healing a tax collector might require, but in this series of events we see that Christ came to heal the corrupted soul *and* the paralyzed body. In these 22 verses, we can know that our Lord prays for broken hearts no less fervently than he prays for those with blocked arteries, that he concerns himself with every disease which causes us pain, whether it be a virus that attacks our lungs or one that corrupts our society. So, while we sometimes see the physical as one thing and the spiritual as another, Jesus sees a link. You can tell that He does, first of all, because when healing the paralyzed man Jesus says, "Son, your sins are forgiven."

He didn't lay his hands on him.

He didn't take his temperature or suggest a remedy.

Nor did he take mud from the ground to rub on the man's skin as he did for the blind man's eyes at the pool of Siloam.

Instead he says, "Son, your sins are forgiven" suggesting that the Savior knew that our bodies and our spirits are connected and that his spiritual sin had something to do with his physical condition. We don't always think this way. We mostly tend to think of maladies that effect our bodies as separate from the state of our souls.

For example, just the other night I broke out in hives. I don't like hives and I really don't like how they keep me up itching until the Benadryl kicks in. For the second time this summer I couldn't sleep for some kind of allergic reaction. I told my doctor about it and he told me to check my diet. Then I told my friend and our Music Director, Dr. Jeffrey Meeks, about it and he told me to relax.

Now those are two different responses - one from a medical doctor, the other from a man with a doctorate in sacred music. Which is it - diet or stress? Does the paralyzed man need a doctor or a savior? Do I need pills or prayer? For this moment in our country's history, do we need Dr. Fauci or Pope Francis?

The true answer is not either/or, for we are spiritual and physical beings. We suffer from conditions which require a liberation from disease and despair. We struggle with symptom and sinfulness. We are confined by physical and spiritual paralysis, and while what we all want, while what we all pray for today is a vaccine, a vaccine can't fix everything.

The way Jesus puts it: "No one sews a piece of unshrunk cloth on an old cloak; otherwise the patch pulls away from it… no one puts new wine into old wineskins; otherwise, the wine will burst the skins." Thinking of this teaching, I say a vaccine is not all that's needed to heal our nation, for this virus is not the only problem we are facing. In fact, this time of quarantine is revealing so many problems in our society that the virus appears to be only the tip of the iceberg.

Certainly, I'm praying for a vaccine. I'm sure you are too, but that's not all we need.

As time goes on and quarantine continues what is revealed are just how many cures our society needs. Think about it. I'm tired of being isolated. But today I realize that many have been living in isolation far before this pandemic hit.

We need a cure for loneliness.

Furthermore, I'm worried about our economy and job loss. I'm worried about all those kids who depended on school lunches. Certainly I'm grateful for the way our school system mobilized to deliver meals to kids in our community and I rejoice for the way our church has gotten involved in feeding people, but poverty and hunger are issues that our country, among the richest nations in the world, has struggled with for generations.

We need a cure for poverty.

This virus reveals so much brokenness that has been with us all along, so in this long lesson from the Gospel of Mark, what I hear is a call from the Lord to not just think about a patch, but a new garment, not new wine in old wine skins, but new wine in new wine skins, a more perfect union, a noble priesthood, a holy people, a new society overcoming the ills that are not new today - just harder to ignore.

We can't go visit at the nursing home today, but it's not as though there was a line out the door to visit our elders before.

Home improvement retailers are reporting record sales as people who don't have anything else to do tackle do-it-yourself projects, but if our concern is only with our own homes than where is our generosity?

Protestors rally in the streets marching for an end to racism today, though it's not as though this were a new problem.

The partisan divide seems greater than ever, but there's no quick fix, no easy solution, because none of us knows how to get along with people who think differently. From sea to shining sea, we all think we're right and they're wrong as cities, towns, and households across these states which were meant to be united are divided.

Fixing our society is no patch job.

A vaccine isn't going to heal all that ails us. So, Christ goes to heal a paralyzed man by forgiving his sins, then he goes to a tax collector and changes his life.

Levi, son of Alphaeus was sitting at the tax booth. Jesus came to him and he, too, got up and walked. Just as Jesus said to the paralyzed man, "Son, your sins are forgiven," this man was made clean and new. He walked away from a life of self-interest. He gave up his vocation where taking advantage of people was required. He stood up from the tax booth, and in so doing he gave up who he had been to become a disciple.

Maybe like me, you can see that our nation needs this kind of miraculous healing as much as we need a vaccine. No longer collecting debts, he invited the Lord and a bunch of other sinners into his house to feed them. No longer focused on what he might take, but on what he might give, his table was open to all kinds of people. So many sinners and tax collectors were sitting in Levi's home with Jesus and his disciples that when the scribes of the Pharisees heard about it, they asked, "Why does he eat with tax collectors and sinners?"

Jesus answered, "Those who are well have no need of a physician, but those who are sick; I have come to call not the righteous but sinners."

Based on what I know of Scribes and Pharisees I want to gently rephrase this statement: "Those who think they are well have no need of a physician, but those who are sick; I have come to call not the self-righteous, but those who know they are sinners."

I rephrase that statement because I believe Jesus is saying that we're all sick.

We just don't necessarily know it.

We're all sinners, we're just afraid to admit it.

Those who are ready to repent are ahead of the game. Therefore, I ask: Are you ready to face the role that you play in our society's brokenness? And are you ready to ask for healing?

Some would say that's the only requirement of being a Christian. It's not so unlike the requirement for entry into Alcoholics Anonymous. All you have to do to become a member is admit that you have a problem that you need help with. And so, all that's required of us who would follow Jesus - to confess that we have a problem with sin that we cannot fix ourselves.

It doesn't matter how we got so sick.

What matters is whether or not we'd let him make us well.

The Psalmist wrote: "As a father has compassion for his children, so the Lord has compassion for those who fear him." That's important in this culture of ours, where in the face of so much brokenness, there are those who double down on their innocence, deny their role in the problem, downplay its severity, blame someone else, or pretend they have it under control.

That's been me.

I don't know what I'm doing, so I've been constantly looking for some assurance that I'm doing this right. I'd love some sign that as a pastor and as a father I'm going to help us all get through to the other side. Now I see that if I've been looking for assurance that I'm doing OK I'm looking for the wrong thing, for what we all must be looking for now is his open hand, calling us to take it and to follow.

*Precious Lord, take my hand;*
*lead me on, help me stand;*
*I am tired, I am weak, I am worn.*
*Through the storm,*
*through the night,*
*lead me on to the light;*
*Take my hand, precious Lord,*
*lead me home.*

Some people have been pretending to be innocent and striving to be perfect for so long they don't know how to do anything else. On this Father's Day, I want to remind you that your heavenly father, maybe unlike your earthly father, doesn't reward perfection with love. That's not even how love works.

Take his hand this day and feel his love.

Our God does not reject sinners but chases after them to eat with them. Just accept his love, for he gives it freely. Take his hand and be made new, that you might become a light in this sin-sick world.

Amen.

www.ingramcontent.com/pod-product-compliance
Lightning Source LLC
Chambersburg PA
CBHW072010110526
44592CB00012B/1256